GOODBYE BUSY
HELLO HAPPY

EDITED BY

PEACE MITCHELL & KATY GARNER

WOMEN CHANGING THE WORLD PRESS

Women Changing the World Press together with KMD Books acknowledges the Elders and Traditonal owners of country throughout Australia and their connection to lands, waters and communities. We pay our respect to Elders past, present and emerging and extend that respect to all Aboriginal and Islander peoples today. We honour more than sixty thousand years of Indigenous women's voices, stories, leadership, wisdom and love.

Edited by Tracy Regan

Typeset in Adobe Garamond Pro 12/17pt

A catalogue record for this
work is available from the
NATIONAL LIBRARY OF AUSTRALIA
National Library of Australia

National Library of Australia Catalogue-in-Publication data:
Goodbye Busy, Hello Happy/Peace Mitchell and Katy Garner

ISBN: 978-0-6455140-6-3
(Paperback)

ISBN: 978-0-6455691-1-7
(Ebook)

This book is for all the women who are overwhelmed, overworked, stressed and exhausted. We knew there had to be a better way to achieve all of your dreams without compromising your health so we brought together women's voices. Women with lived experience, women with expertise and women who would help to guide you as you navigate and unhook from the glorification of busy to create a life that feels as good as it looks.

Peace & Katy

CONTENTS

FOREWORD

Dr Kristy Goodwin

In a world where 'busyness' is revered and seen as a benchmark of success, it takes courage and a radical shift in our thinking and ways of being to stop worshipping at the altar of hustle. Yet for people who take bold steps and stop believing that being busy is a necessary prerequisite and a hallmark of success, the rewards are immense ... and are probably a reflection of 'real' success.

This book shares the powerful stories and firsthand experiences that led people to ditch being busy and dismantle the hustle and grind culture that permeates our modern, digital world. You'll read the anecdotes and changes (some of them quite significant) to embrace a life that's free from the burden of being busy. You'll be inspired by the stories and insights about how removing the shackles of being busy has resulted in not only a more sustainable lifestyle, but one that's simultaneously brought more joy and contentment to those who stopped wearing busyness as a badge of honour. You'll be inspired by people who were brave enough to pivot the modern paradigms that define what 'success' *really* looks like.

In a world where many of us are now knowledge workers (people who spend the majority of their workdays using digital technologies such as laptops and computers to perform their work), we often don't have tangible measures of our output. Unlike tradespeople or caring occupations, who do have clear output indicators, knowledge workers don't have concrete evidence of their efforts. Cal Newport, in his book *Deep Work,* suggests that, 'In the absence of clear indicators of what it means to be productive and valuable in their jobs, many knowledge workers turn back toward an industrial indicator of productivity: doing lots of stuff in a visible manner.' As a result, we revert to industrialised models of productivity, where time is a metric of our performance and having visual indicators of our productivity is essential. We revert to being busy.

Many of us have bought into the vernacular that in order to be perceived as being productive and successful we have to be seen to be visibly busy. So we fill our calendars with meetings, we spend countless hours sending and receiving emails, we're on a hamster wheel of group chats and Teams/Slack notifications. We look for overt, tangible measures – visual indicators – that signal busyness and therefore imply that we're being productive.

However, having days dominated by busywork leaves many people feeling stressed, overwhelmed and burnt-out, as this is often at the expense of the important, needle-moving work we should be accomplishing. Many people today lament the fact that they don't have enough time for deep, focused work.

This is leading to increased stress, and if left unresolved, prolonged stress can lead to burnout. Burnout is rampant. Recent research from the *2021 Global Burnout Study*[1] confirmed that 34.7% of people have symptoms of burnout.

However, being busy is not serving us. Instead, being busy is enslaving us to outdated and unhelpful paradigms, where being busy is a marker of your productivity.

---

1 infinite-potential.com.au/2021-global-burnout-study

Busyness is often seen as a status symbol and an indicator of success. However, being perpetually busy is at odds with peak performance. It's out of alignment with how we ideally need to perform as humans: it's incongruent with our biological blueprint.

Digital technologies were touted as the silver bullet that were supposed to make us more productive and efficient. However, the productivity paradox confirms that what has transpired is the opposite. The productivity gains we were *supposed* to reap from new technologies have not resulted. Instead, we're *not* more productive. If anything, people are more busy and stressed than they've ever been and *not* as productive as once hoped.

Why? Our digital behaviours and habits are some of the chief culprits that have led many of us to busy but not necessarily productive lives. Our digital ways of working are out of alignment with our biological blueprint. For example, technology has fuelled our 'always-on' mentality that has prompted people to feel like they always need to be busy – we can respond to emails at our kids' soccer game, we can be out for dinner with our family but taking a work call. We tell ourselves we need to reply to an email (even if it's Sunday at 3pm). Digitalisation has created a pervasive culture of twenty-four seven, always-on accessibility that has eroded the boundary between where work ends and our personal lives begin. Technology has obliterated any work-life boundaries we once enjoyed. This always-on approach creates fatigue, exhaustion and unhappiness and is unsustainable.

We also know that the digital intensity of our days has increased in recent years thanks to remote and now hybrid work. Microsoft data[2] confirms that our workday spans have increased by 13%, we're spending more time in virtual meetings (we've seen a 252% increase in meeting time since February 2020) and a 32% increase in chats (of which 28% of these are now occurring after-hours). We're processing more and more digital data, and our brains have a finite cognitive capacity. This is why many of us

2 microsoft.com/en-us/worklab/work-trend-index/great-expectations-making-hybrid-work-work

are experiencing 'infobesity' and feel like we need to be busy to keep up with the constant digital demands. This is resulting in digital depletion and playing a role in why so many people feel burnt-out and unhappy.

This constant onslaught of digital information has nudged many of us to adopt some unhealthy work practices that are in conflict with our biology. For example, we now know that many people are working late at night. Microsoft are referring to this as the 'triple peak day' where there are now three productivity peaks in our workdays, where we once traditionally saw two peaks (usually at 10am and another at 2pm). Now we're seeing a third peak at 10pm! This is workday creep. As humans, we're not designed to work long hours. In fact, our prefrontal cortex, the part of our brain that helps with logical thinking, problem-solving and analytical thinking, only has four to six hours of battery life per day (pardon the pun). We're not designed to be working in marathons. We're biologically designed to work in sprints, especially when working online.

We also know that our increased digital load has encouraged many people to spend their days multitasking. We sit in virtual meetings, clearing our inboxes. We jump from task to task throughout the day. Not only does this perpetual cycle of busy put a dent in our productivity (we know, for example, that multitasking increases our error rates and increases task duration), but it also has a negative effect on our wellbeing (it leaves us feeling depleted as our brains burn through glucose when multitasking and release cortisol, leaving us feeling stressed).

In our quest to be productive, many of us spend our days going from task to task being busy. We go from our inbox, to a meeting, back to our inbox – with a constant pulse of busyness. We don't take breaks. Yet working online is mentally taxing. Brain scans show, for example, that ten-minute buffer breaks between virtual meetings can significantly reduce cortisol – stress hormones – in the brain. However, many of us, in our pursuit of being busy, rarely include buffer breaks. So yet again, we're busy being busy and not working in optimal ways.

Now is the time to question whether we want to perpetuate the dominant culture of busyness. Given that the pandemic has forced many people to question how, where and when they work (and their life and values more broadly), now is an ideal time to scrutinise if we want to continue to be busy at the expense of our wellbeing and happiness (and our performance).

Or do we, as the authors in the forthcoming pages will share, seek new perspectives and paradigms? Do we find better ways of working that don't revere busyness? Do we redefine what real success looks like and find ways of working that work for us and make us happy in the process? I suggest we take this opportunity to find better ways of working that are matched to our biological needs. In doing so, we'll boost our happiness and also be more productive.

IDENTITY LOST, IDENTITY FOUND

Amanda Thompson

My grandfather – or Pap, as we used to call him – was a man who refused to be defined by a stereotype. You might even say he rebelled against it.

Pap was born with a congenital eye disease. At birth, they said he would lose his eyesight completely quite early in life. In a cruel twist of fate, he was just six years old when he was hit in the eye with a stone, which escalated the disease, and he became totally blind.

Pap was a man who refused to be defined by his disability. As a child, I never thought of him as disabled. He never let being blind hold him back and would resist attempts by society to place limits on who he was. In society's eyes, he was blind. Yet in his eyes, he was able to see – and he saw so much more than you or I could ever imagine.

Even though he was blind for pretty much all his years, he lived a fulfilling life. He met and married my grandma and had two children and five grandchildren. He studied and became a barrister before braille university books even existed. Like a true Victorian, he loved the football and never missed watching a game. He would often shout out that the umpire needed glasses. That always made me laugh. To me, he saw and experienced life in the same way I did. And I was able to see him that way because that's how he saw himself.

Watching the way Pap moved through life was a masterclass in how to reject being defined by how others see you. If you define yourself through the lens of how others perceive you, you can lose sight of who you really are. You can lose your true identity.

Even though I was exposed to this lesson early in life through my pap, it's a lesson that has taken me many, many years to learn. I still don't always master it. It sounds like such an easy piece of advice to follow – don't define yourself by stereotypes. But it's actually quite hard to not see yourself the way others do.

When we're kids, we're not burdened with this pressure. We like what we like, and we don't particularly care what others think. We're so much better at seeking out the experiences that bring us joy. We're in tune with our real selves. When I was at school, I wasn't a girly girl nor was I a tomboy, and I was completely satisfied with that. I was happy with just being me and not fitting a mould. Somehow, as we age, we begin to unlearn this. Eventually we succumb to judgement, stereotypes and assumptions. We can forget how to understand ourselves without filtering it through the lens of somebody else's perspective. This is a sure-fire way to become completely detached from your identity.

There have been several times in my life when I have felt disconnected from who I really am, where my identity eroded to a point where I no longer knew who I was anymore. This was the case when I was twenty-four and going for a run one day. Little did I know, that unremarkable event would take a terrible turn. As I made my way home, I was running along the fence of a primary school, just metres from my house. Without warning, I was brutally attacked and sexually assaulted by a stranger, in what would later be determined to be a calculated attack. It left me physically and emotionally battered and bruised. I had black eyes and cuts and grazes on my face. But the most horrific pain inflicted was the pain that couldn't be seen. I was determined not to let this man stop me from living my life. I wanted to put it behind me and focus on the good in my life. In hindsight, I was internalising my grief and putting on a brave face. Instead of properly processing what happened, I pushed on.

This was one of those times where, without realising it, I became disconnected from my identity. In an effort to cast off the label of 'rape victim', I threw myself into a new career as a financial planner and a new relationship with a man who would later become my husband. But this alone wouldn't help me rediscover myself. A part of me was still lost because I was still living with unprocessed fear, guilt, shame, sadness and terror. I had just pushed it way down inside so I didn't have to experience those difficult emotions. And in the process, I began to lose sight of myself.

A decade later, after getting married and having two children, I made the difficult decision to end my marriage and start life as a single mum. I was racked with self-doubt. I knew it was the right decision, but I worried about my daughters. There was a lot of uncertainty, and I didn't know where I was going in life. There was also another loss of identity as I felt the stigma of being a single mum. I know I shouldn't have let it bother me. Who really cares? After all, it was my decision. But the truth is, I did care. I cared that others judged me because of it. And even though the decision would ultimately help me reclaim my true identity, at that confusing time, more than anything, I just felt lost.

Only a few months after I separated from my husband, I got so sick that I almost died. My heart was struggling to beat. The doctors told me I had had a heart attack – at just thirty-four years old. Worse yet, the doctors were baffled that my heart was still beating; they couldn't believe I was still alive! In retrospect, there were signs that I had ignored, like fatigue and vomiting. At the time I was working so hard and in the middle of a separation, so I chalked it up to stress. I was so disconnected from my physical and emotional self that I didn't realise something was seriously wrong.

Two years later I was diagnosed with melanoma. Suddenly I was the 'cancer patient'. This was another chip away at my identity. I didn't feel like me; I felt like someone else. The uncertainty of the diagnosis completely unnerved me. I've always believed that if you want something bad enough and if you work hard enough, you'll succeed. But cancer doesn't work that way, and that scared me. I was determined not to let cancer stop me from living my life, and so, in what I now know was an attempt to maintain control and distract from the emotional pain, I signed up for my first ironman event. It would turn out to be one of the best things I ever did, but not in the ways I expected.

There is a saying about triathlon: 'Halfway through the marathon out in the ironman, you find yourself stripped bare for all to see.' What I discovered, unexpectedly, was a way to find myself again – to rebuild my identity piece by piece.

Triathlon training is tough. You become so physically depleted that you actually lose a lot of mental strength. In my case, the walls I had carefully built, year after year, to keep my emotions at bay, began to tumble down. I had no choice but to start opening up to myself. I confronted the fear I had about cancer, the guilt I felt around some of the decisions I made as a mother, the self-doubt about leaving my husband and the uncertainty of not knowing where I was going in life.

Triathlon gave me the calm and focus to just move forward, one foot in front of the other, but without trying to outrun my experiences or emotions. It forced me to process those emotions – something I hadn't been able to do for many years.

A triathlon swim is the perfect metaphor for the challenges we face in life. Swimming against powerful and relentless waves can feel like one stroke forward, ten strokes back. You have no choice but to take on the waves. Slowly inching forward, you finally reach that first buoy and turn to start swimming across the waves. If you persevere and make it to that final buoy out in the ocean, then the waves that have been your worst enemy become your best friend as you ride them into shore. Ironman taught me that resilience is more than just pushing forward – you have to face the waves head-on in order to make it back to the beach.

In this time, I began to reconnect with what my grandfather taught me all those years ago. I had a life-changing realisation that how people perceive me isn't who I truly am. My identity is forged by me, not by anyone else. I began to shed the identities people had imposed on me: 'single mum', 'cancer survivor', 'ex-wife' or 'rape victim.' I was rediscovering who I really was and finding my true identity again.

I began to tune in to my intuition and trust myself again. I began to understand myself better by asking myself some very important questions:

What gets me excited?

What gives me purpose?

What is most important to me?

What mark do I want to leave on this world?

Answering these questions, I found my identity again.

The physical and emotional self are interconnected. When we're in touch with our physical self, we're in touch with our emotional self. If you have a feeling that won't go away, take the time to understand what that feeling is telling you. It could be goosebumps or recurring dreams. For me, it's butterflies. I've felt this with all the major decisions and exciting leaps of faith in my life, like starting my business or having children. Something in my gut knew that starting my own business was the right call and would become part of who I am. The same goes for motherhood. I was listening to advice from the person who knows me best – myself. Don't ignore that feeling, lean into it. It's usually a cue that whatever is evoking that physical reaction is an expression of your true self.

My pap was blind, but he saw more clearly than most. He saw life in such a special and unique way. He never let challenges or obstacles stop him from succeeding. He knew who he was and refused to be defined by stereotypes. We should all do the same.

You are the person you see in the mirror. You are the person you see in your heart. Only you, the people you love and the people who love you really know who you are. Today, I see myself as mum – not a single mum, but just a mum – I see myself as a business owner, an athlete, a good friend and a caring daughter. On a good day, I see myself as strong and brave. But once again, I see myself as just me, just Amanda. And that is more than enough. I hope when you look in the mirror you see just you – not a stereotype – but a wonderful, unique, special and loved *you*.

AMANDA THOMPSON

Amanda Thompson is an award-winning financial planner, ironwoman and the founder and director of Endurance Financial. Whether she's launching her own business, facing a cancer battle or qualifying three times for the Ironman World Championships, Amanda has never been afraid of a challenge.

Amanda specialises in offering strategic financial guidance for individuals and businesses with complex matters requiring more than textbook advice. She is particularly driven to help women overcome the gender biases that stand in the way of personal achievement; lessons learned after thriving in typically male-dominated environments.

Amanda's areas of expertise include money mindset, small business goal-setting and strategy, along with the 'traditional' financial planning skills of investment strategy, wealth creation, self-managed superannuation, personal insurance and retirement strategies. Her areas of focus in life include resilience, determination and dedication to something bigger than self.

Her *Financially Fit Women* program has been designed to give women business owners a clear understanding of how to make their organisation profitable, pay themselves what they're worth and achieve their long-term financial goals. The course empowers participants to build confidence, overcome any limiting beliefs and develop a positive relationship with their finances, while arming them with the insights they need to take positive action in their business.

Website: endurancefinancial.com.au

YOUR HOME IS YOUR SANCTUARY

DESIGNING YOUR HOME SO THAT IT SUPPORTS YOU

Amy Kennedy

I support a lot of families and women; primarily intelligent, successful women who are wonderful mothers or kicking goals in their career and other areas of their lives – often both.

They all appear to have everything held together. The perfect, happy life. But often, what lies beyond the front door of their home tells a different story.

They are busy. They are overworked, overwhelmed and simply exhausted. Most would describe themselves as organised people, or at least they were at one point in time, before some form of change rocked their world. They may be facing immense pressure in their daily lives. Others are silently dealing with anxiety, depression or a chronic health concern. Some have had an exciting new arrival to the family or a tragic loss. Others may be learning how to negotiate a recent diagnosis of ADHD or a life-changing illness.

Most are also overwhelmed by their home, often finding it challenging to complete what they perceive to be simple everyday cleaning or life admin tasks. Some are constantly misplacing their belongings, others habitually late to meetings or have trouble paying their bills on time despite having the finances available. They often find difficulty in maintaining the order of their home in the way that they would like.

They are stuck and seeking change, but are unsure how to achieve it. The common thread amongst all these women is that their home is not supporting them in the way they need.

This chaos or disorganisation in their home adds a considerable amount of additional pressure and stress for these women and their families. At the end of a busy, stressful or demanding day at work, from the moment they walk into the front door of their home, more chaos hits them right in the face. The thought of more tasks, more responsibility and more decisions is unbearable.

They are not happy. Some are barely coping and others are not. It's debilitating.

The good news is our home doesn't need to be chaotic or demanding. Our home can be a sanctuary, a safe space where we can escape the pressures of our working life and a space to give our brains and bodies a rest.

The environment in which we live can have a major and positive influence on our levels of anxiety, happiness and sense of self-control. Research states that excess clutter in our homes negatively impacts both our physical and mental health in rather severe ways. It can contribute to a sense of shame, lead to low self-esteem as well as having a negative impact on our relationships. [1]

We want to be in a position where we are controlling our home and our life. The unfortunate thing is that, for many, our home and other inanimate items within our home are controlling us. They control the look, feel and smell of our home, as well as the way we, as individuals, feel and function. With the uncertainty of the world around us and so many variables in our lives that we are unable to control, our home is the one area where we can have full control and the ownership to set it up in

---

[1]   Choosi: Clutter Report 2017, CoreData, Australia, viewed 23 June 2022, <https://www.choosi.com.au/documents/choosi-clutter-report-whitepaper.pdf>

the way that we need and like.

If we pare back our belongings to those items that we genuinely use each day and the things that we love and are passionate about, we automatically reduce the number of decisions we need to make daily. We also dramatically reduce the amount of time and effort we need to maintain a tidy home.

Think about a morning where you don't need to make any decisions. You wake up and put on your favourite slippers. You wash and prepare yourself for the day with products that nourish and suit your skin and leave you feeling good. The products you have tried along the way that didn't feel right were discarded the moment you realised they weren't right for you. There is no trigger of wasted money or guilt of an unused product that, deep down, you know you are never going to use.

You open your wardrobe and can see everything you own. You pull out any outfit. You don't need to spend time thinking about what you will wear today. It doesn't really matter which items you choose, as you know that everything in your wardrobe works with each other, is flattering and fits you perfectly. You pop it on and immediately feel special; your very best self. You no longer put up with uncomfortable or unflattering clothing. You only wear the things that are comfortable and make you feel good every single day.

You go to the kitchen. You make a cup of coffee or tea and take joy in drinking out of your favourite mug and eat your breakfast using your favourite bowls and plates. You are using the good stuff normally reserved for special celebrations and it makes you feel just a little bit special.

You get the kids ready for school without fuss. You are not feeling the anxious pressure you often feel when time is ticking, with the knowledge that you need to get out of the door quickly to ensure you are not late. You are calm and happy.

As you leave your home, you put on your favourite shoes and quickly grab your handbag, mobile phone and keys. The morning runs smoothly and calmly. You even have time for your journalling and morning mediation if you chose to. You leave your home happy.

Never at any point during the morning are you left looking for things you have misplaced. Everything was in its rightful place. You didn't waste time making decisions on what to wear today, what mug to use or even what to eat for breakfast. You weren't hunting for your child's library book or a missing shoe. Your emotions remained regulated. Everything was there and ready to go. You are happy.

Does this scenario seem a little far-fetched? Like a fantasy world? Or something that is only achievable for those with the budget for a live-in nanny or daily house cleaner?

Maybe – but the fact is, this scenario is achievable and realistic for everyone.

It doesn't need to take a lot of time, energy or effort to maintain a home when you have pared back your belongings to what you truthfully use each day. It surprisingly takes a lot less time to have a tidy home than you might think when you remove all the obstacles.

HOW DO WE ACHIEVE THIS?

Ensure you have a goal for your home and lifestyle

Understand what it is you would like your home and life to feel like. What is your vision and focus? What activities do you love and need to do in each room of your home? Fully understanding how you want your spaces to function can help you design and organise a home that fully supports you and your lifestyle and gives you permission to let go of the obstacles and those things that you don't need.

You need less than you think to make you happy

It's not the things in our life that makes us happy. Our level of happiness generally doesn't change much when we purchase a new car or handbag, at least not for the long-term, once the endorphins released from making the new purchase have subsided. Research has found that it's the things that relate to our wellbeing, including our social connections, time to do the things that we enjoy doing, our health and having adequate sleep, that make us happiest in life. [2]

Place higher emphasis on the value of time

I like my clients to look at each item in their home with respect to the time they spend using the item, not the monetary value. Holding onto unused or rarely used items can take up a lot of your valuable time. It's true that you may have spent a lot of money on a particular item, but if you're not using it, it doesn't matter how much of your hard-earned cash you spent on it, it's not adding any value to your life. Rather, it's making your life today more complicated. Time to get it out, time to put it away, time to care for and maintain it and most commonly time to move it out of the way to get to the items that you actually need and use. That is lot of time and energy to dedicate to something you are not using. To put it simply, the more you own, the more your home demands of you. You can eliminate all the extra work by simply removing the item from your home. The less you have, the less your home demands of you. So how much is your time worth to you?

Less things doesn't mean less soul, less heart or less warmth

By having less, it allows you to showcase and enjoy the things that you love and adore and creates more room for spontaneity, fun and play. Having less things in your home provides room for you to create your own sanctuary or creative space – your own special abode. You can have as much in your home as you need or desire, but if your belongings begin to interrupt your ability to complete your day-to-day tasks or make it

2   Professor Laurie Santos, Department of Psychology 2022, The Science of Well-Being Course, Yale University via Coursera, viewed April 2022, https://www.coursera.org/learn/the-science-of-well-being

difficult for you to use the space in the way you desire, then it may mean you have an excess problem, which inadvertently may be making your life more complicated than it needs be.

Organise your home in a way that makes sense to you

Everyone is different. There is no right way to organise a space – in fact, the right way is what makes sense for you. This is crucial. The more tailored the organising system, that is, the more it suits your individual preferences, sensory or processing modalities – the unique way your brain thinks and the positive habits and routines that you have already established over your lifetime – then the more likely the organising system will be successful, with a greater chance you will be able to maintain it for a longer term. A cookie-cutter approach to organising is rarely sustainable. Pretty baskets, containers and cute labels are just one tiny tool in the organising process. A tiny process I love, but in my professional experience, simply putting items into containers or baskets without considering your goals and individual tendencies can lead to additional chaos and disorganisation. Much like adequately proving your dough when baking bread is a crucial step, skipping it can lead to failure or an unsatisfactory result. Heading straight to the shops to buy stylish containers can be an easy way to make it look more aesthetically pleasing or to hide the mess, but it doesn't necessarily make your home more organised.

There is always a solution that can be tailored to every family's unique idiosyncrasies. Problem-solving and thinking outside the box is one of my favourite parts of being a professional organiser. That, and being able to support my clients to make lasting change.

You need less storage space than you think

It is easy to feel like we need more storage when our wardrobes and drawers are overflowing. Often, our storage spaces are filled to the brim with things we no longer use or need. In many cases, we don't even remember what we own.

Meanwhile, all the things we use regularly don't have a dedicated storage space within the home. When we stand back and objectively look at the things we value, it is sad and somewhat wasteful to realise that, often, the things we treasure and use the most are the things that are cared for the least. They are the items left lying around on the kitchen table, bench or even the floor, whilst the things we never use or don't remember we even own, are tucked away beautifully and safe in our cupboards.

In most cases, the problem isn't that we don't have enough storage space, it's that we've got too many things. We are holding onto things that were once important but no longer hold any relevance for the lifestyle we want to live today. Once we've pared back to the items that genuinely support the lifestyle we want, suddenly, we have more than enough storage in our homes. In fact, we probably have too much storage. Shelves and sometimes whole cupboards are left bare.

We are not talking changing to a minimalist lifestyle (although that is fabulous if you choose to), we are talking about removing the excess. You will still have ample possessions to live a very comfortable life and continue to do everything you want, while having the home styled the way you like. But you will have simply pared back to the things you use regularly, the things that you love and make you happy and the things that support your passions and hobbies – the things you love to do and share with your family and friends.

Simply reducing the amount of items you own, in a way that marries with your goals for your life and home, can have a profound and meaningful effect in your life and happiness. This will include building strong organising systems with respect to your sensibilities, functioning strengths, learning styles, habits and routines.

A home that is considered and organised in a way that works for you, and supports you in the way that you need it to, can lead to amazing things. It's truly life-changing. I've seen women emerge from periods of deep overwhelm, depression or anxiety to find a new sense of confidence, calm and happiness. You know the kind of happiness that makes you glow? The new-found space in their home and release on their mental load is profound. They begin making big decisions that have been weighing on them for years. Some take on new passions and hobbies, many have started their own business, begun studying or returned to the workforce in a way they never thought they could achieve. They have found themselves again. They are proud. They are happy.

They have created their sanctuary simply by designing a home that supports them. And that is pure happiness.

AMY KENNEDY

Amy Kennedy is a practical and fun-loving professional organiser and coach who gets a buzz from supporting others to organise their home and life.

Amy founded The Organising Bee – a professional home organising and decluttering service based in Canberra, Australia – in 2015 out of a desire to create a service that truly added value to the lives of others. Since then, her professional life has been devoted to supporting women and their families to ease the pressures of everyday life by reclaiming their space and time.

Amy provides one-to-one, hands-on support to organise and establish systems in her clients' homes, coupled with virtual and face-to-face consulting and coaching. Amy offers a client-centric approach when organising a home with a key emphasis on guiding and teaching the client organisational and time management strategies, so at the end of the project the client not only has a beautifully organised and functional space but has new tools and strategies to help them to stay organised for longer. Amy has supported hundreds of busy families to learn, grow and blossom into their own version of success, something many had never dreamed possible.

Amy enjoys running workshops and speaking publicly to educate others about home organisation, decluttering, clutter-free living and time management. Amy also offers self-paced online courses through her website.

Amy is respected within the Australian professional organising industry, and acknowledging the five-star reviews received from clients on the Houzz platform, Amy has led The Organising Bee to win the Best of Houzz Service award for five consecutive years (2017–2021).

Amy is committed to ongoing professional development, has a keen interest in productivity and time management and is currently on a mission to learn as many different techniques as possible to support her clients with differing functioning strengths to build sustainable and positive habits.

Since graduating with a Bachelor of Communication from the University of Canberra in 2000, Amy has completed specialist hoarding training through Hoarding Home Solutions, Australia (2020), has obtained a Specialist Certificate of Residential Organizing (2019) from the National Association of Productivity & Organizing Professionals University, United States, along with completing a number of community-based interior design and positive psychology courses. Amy is also currently training to become a certified ADHD and productivity coach with Coach Approach for Organizers approved coach-specific training per the International Coach Federation (ICF). Amy is also a professional member of the Institute of Professional Organisers (IOPO) and the National Association of Productivity & Organizing Professionals (NAPO).

Amy is highly active in her local community, holding a variety of executive positions on local community and school committees. In her spare time, you'll find Amy with her family, hugging a warm coffee with a good book or perusing the pages of her favourite magazine, *Home Beautiful.*

Website: organisingbee.com.au
Facebook: organisingbee
Instagram: @organisingbee
LinkedIn: amykennedyprofessionalorganiser

THE BUSYNESS PARADOX

HOW TO BREAK IT SO YOU CAN LIVE A HAPPY LIFE

Ange Fragiacomo

'It's not enough to be busy, so are the ants.
The question is, what are you busy about?'
Henry David Thoreau

Most would say we are lucky to live in a modern world where everything has been engineered to make our lives easier. Think fast food, the evolution of cars, washing machines, instant hot water. Everywhere you look, the world is full of modern gadgets and conveniences to make life easier. But there are also some disadvantages that come with this fast-paced world.

That feeling of rushing through the day, constantly being pressed for time and always 'on', has never been a more accepted and unavoidable aspect of our lives. Everywhere you turn, there is yet another sign that a busy life is a good life. Speed is highly regarded, efficiency praised, and the ability to juggle multiple tasks is applauded. Busyness has become the new normal, and it's no surprise you feel compelled to always be busy.

To make things trickier, when our fast-paced world does suddenly become interrupted, negative feelings of frustration, anxiety and discomfort tend to surface. This busyness paradox is exactly why this conversation needs to be had. It's time to lean into these mixed signals and unpack how you can break it so you can live a happy life.

I'm here to show you that it really is possible. All you need to do is trust the process. Trust that the world you live in is not going to fall apart if you slow down. Trust that the people who rely on you will still thrive, even if you take some time out for yourself. It really is possible to say goodbye to that busy feeling and hello to a life that makes you happy.

So, let's first explore why you are drawn to a busy life in the first place.

THE SCIENCE

When you complete tasks, your brain releases the pleasure hormone dopamine – a neurotransmitter that is responsible for generating feelings of accomplishment, satisfaction and happiness. This release of dopamine makes you feel good and motivates you to continue completing tasks. You get hooked on this feeling and seek repetition. So, you add more and more to your to-do list.

THE GUILT

You have grown up in a society where a high value is placed on productivity. It has become the norm to feel and think that the more you do, the more you are worth. You associate busy with success, and you feel pressure to constantly be busy. To make things worse, emotions such as guilt, shame and worry can be triggered when you relax and do nothing. Which leads you to start doing things again.

FEAR OF MISSING OUT (FOMO)

You pack your schedule to bursting point due to FOMO or the fear of not being included in something you see others doing. Social media has intensified this issue thanks to your ability to scroll through other people's life events. FOMO releases negative emotions like loneliness and boredom, so to quash these emotions you say 'yes' to everything, which makes your life even busier.

DREAM BIG

You grew up in a home where you were encouraged to dream big. You learnt that the world was your oyster and you could become anything you wanted – if you worked for it. You could have it all: a successful career, happy marriage, children, a life of travel. This was a great mantra to live by, until you ran out of time in your day.

Which ones resonate with you the most? I can relate to all of them, especially the last one. I loved the idea that I could become anything I wanted to be, *if I worked for it.* So, I set about creating this life for myself, seeing how much I could cram in. The more I did, the more adrenaline ran through me, and I found myself craving more and saying 'yes' to more. I never put much thought into the 'why', I just took advantage of the fact that I could dream big! Unfortunately, for me and many others, our desire to live a busy, fulfilling life sets us on a path that is impossible to maintain.

My breaking point came at a time when there were a lot of good things happening in my world. I was happily married with three beautiful kids, I owned my own business and I was still playing competitive sport. But my body was starting to say 'enough'. I was burning the wick at both ends and my ability to stay well was being constantly tested. Around the same time, my mum was diagnosed with terminal cancer, and like many others faced with news like this, I entered autopilot. My world shifted and I juggled it all without any regard for my own wellbeing. This was compounded further by the overwhelm that engulfed me, knowing my mum was embarking on one of the toughest fights of her life, one that she would not win.

You most likely have your own burnout story or some awareness that your current way of being is not serving you; living a busy life is costing you more than it is benefitting you. Your wellbeing, work-life disharmony and meaningless relationships create a ripple effect on you and those around you.

What this time showed me was that I needed a reboot. I was both physically and emotionally spent. Being constantly on the go was not serving me. I knew it was time to question why I was walking the path I was on, and ultimately, whether I was happy on this path.

So, I went on a journey and became my own experiment. At times, I nailed life and at other times, I failed miserably. But each time I failed, I would pause and revisit how I had got to this place again. I got really good at asking, *Is this adding value to my life?* and, *What parts of my life can I make more efficient?* Over time I got better at both. My busy no longer leaves me feeling overwhelmed and it includes lots of things that make me happy. Now it's time for you to do the same.

SAY HELLO TO HAPPY

'Never get so busy making a living, that you forget to make a life.'
Anonymous

This is where the fun begins! It's time to recalibrate your emotional compass and gain clarity around what your true north looks like, what emotions you want to feel more of and what activities make you happy. This state of utopia will be different for each of you, but what will remain the same is that when you take the time to tune in to what makes you happy, you give yourself a greater chance of creating a life that brings you joy.

Which feelings make you happy?

Happiness is an emotional state characterised by pleasant or positive feelings. Most people associate feeling joyful with happiness, but what people don't realise is there are many levels to happiness, including contentment, fulfilment and satisfaction – along the way to joy.

From the list below pick three to five emotions that allow you to experience a state of happiness. If a different word springs to mind for you, add it to the list. As an example, I know I am happiest when I feel calm, valued or energised.

Admiration	Affection	Amusement	Awe	Cheerfulness
Complete	Confident	Contentment	Curious	Energised
Enjoyment	Enthusiasm	Fulfilment	Gratitude	Hope
Inspired	Joy	Love	Optimism	Pleased
Pride	Satisfaction	Serenity	Valued	

Which activities make you happy?

Now make a list of all the things you do that make you happy. It doesn't matter if you are currently doing them or not. Simply list everything you wish you had time for. If you are in a state of busy and having trouble thinking of something, try to identify activities you like doing under each of these headings:

- Connecting with others (including family).
- Being active.
- Learning new things.
- Being aware of your surroundings.
- Helping others.
- Taking time to rest and relax.

Now let's combine the two. Take one of the emotions you want to feel more of and list the activities from your list that allow that emotion to surface. As an example, when I want to feel calm, the following activities work for me. You might even like to add a third column that highlights your why.

Emotion	Activity	Why
Calm	Get outdoors	The sight of water calms me. A long walk clears my mind.
	Declutter	Mess overwhelms me.
	Listen to music	Helps me feel centred.

Hopefully you are starting to see what happiness really means to you and the types of activities you can add into your life to help you rediscover your true north. Remember, it will be different for everyone. You may feel calm when you are drinking a cup of tea, talking to a friend on the phone or lying down in a dark room. There are no right or wrong scenarios to this – it's simply whatever aligns for you.

Now place these words somewhere you can see them every day. Whenever you reach a state of busy, refer to your new-found emotional compass and use it to redirect your time and attention. Especially when deciding what you should say yes to and what you should say no to. Over time you will not need a visual cue, the things you value will become imprinted on your mind.

SAY GOODBYE TO BUSY

'Creating space by getting rid of things that no longer serve you invites possibility, opportunity and more space for love.'
Miranda Anderson

Unschedule

The easiest way to create space in your life is to reassess the weeks ahead. What have you said yes to that is not going to serve you? It's time to be brave and remove these items from your schedule and start saying no to other things. You don't need a reason to say no. But this is an important first step in allowing you to make room for things that matter to you.

Refuel

Now it's time to review your sleep, nutrition and exercise habits, because when you refuel, regaining the brainpower to tackle the reason you got here in the first place (being too busy) quickly follows.

You may not be able to focus on all of them right away – i.e. you might be a new mum breastfeeding every three hours, so getting more sleep is tricky. But you can still make changes, and remember, even the smallest shifts will help. Things like focusing on drinking more water or going for a stroll with your newborn will help you reset. Write down at least two things you can start or stop doing that will help your body thrive. Focus on this for a few days and you will start to think more clearly.

Reflect

Now it's time to reflect on the real issue. Why are you feeling the way that you are? Note down all the scenarios in your life that are currently adding to your busyness. Is it work? Is it the constant run-around you do for your kids? Perhaps it's the number of things you need to get done before you leave for work. For every scenario you have identified, give yourself a busyness score out of ten. With one being calm and ten so busy you can't figure out what task to do first.

Dive deeper

Select the scenario with the highest 'busy' score and dive a bit deeper. Write down all the things that are causing you to feel the way you do.

If you chose work, is it the pile of unanswered emails? The report you need to finish? The number of meetings each day? Keep jotting things down until you can't think of anything else. Now identify two things that you can start doing straightaway that will help you feel less busy. It could be that you allocate time in your diary to work on your report or you could condense all your meetings into one part of your day.

Now let's look at things you could stop doing. The reason we want to remove things from your list is that right now your brain doesn't have the space to attract new things into your life that make you happy. You're just too stuck in *busy*.

Maybe your biggest pressure point is running your kids around to their activities. Why not consider teaming up with another parent to share the drop-offs and pick-ups? Imagine what you could do with an extra thirty minutes if you were sharing the load. Speak up, start the conversation, as every half-hour counts, and the parent you share with will also appreciate getting some time back in their day.

Act

Put the plan into action. Make sure you give it a good go, and after a couple of weeks, pause and note how it made you feel. Did it work? Did you feel less busy in that part of your day? Or was it a fail? Did it create bigger stress elsewhere? If it was a fail, that's okay too. Note it down. Accept it was a bump in the road and try again. The key is to try different things until you find your ways to say *goodbye to busy*.

You can then say yes to things that make you feel happier. Maybe it's that cup of tea and a chat with a friend. Maybe it's an early morning walk. Whatever activities you noted down earlier, these are the things that you now need to consciously add back into your life.

But start slow – only add a couple of things at a time. I want you to succeed, and when you chunk it down into small manageable tasks, you can master these changes before you take on more.

Life has also shown me that it takes time and energy to create a life that truly aligns to your happiness goals and brings you true joy. Life is full of curveballs, so even with our greatest intentions of living in a state where we can feel happy, we will also experience phases when life still seems out of control. If we can continuously take the time to adjust, we will be in a better position to respond to the bumps in the road and recognise when the pendulum is swinging the wrong way.

For me, I find I go through this process two to four times a year, usually as the seasons change. This is when I find my commitments alter and my energy levels shift, so I need to do a bit of a reset. This same rhythm may work for you, or you may find that once a year is enough. Regardless, I hope I have sparked something inside you, along with the other amazing women who have shared their stories in this book, to get you into the driver's seat on your path to happiness. You now have a whole new suite of resources available that will allow you to make the small changes you need in your life, to say goodbye to the busy and hello to the happy. xox

ANGE FRAGIACOMO

With an undergraduate degree in applied science (human movement), my wellbeing foundation started here, and I spent my early years fine-tuning my knowledge and skills in the areas of nutrition, physiology and psychology. Twenty-plus years in the workforce then showed me that to feel truly well, physical health was not enough. Only when you have the right mindset and habits in each key area of your life – career, relationships, health, emotional, finance and rest – can you truly bloom. My learning journey continued, allowing me to become the mindset and wellbeing coach I am today.

I am continually expanding my knowledge base. Most recently completing an MBA unit in workplace wellbeing to ensure I can best support my clients in this ever-changing world and so that I can also actively contribute to helping organisations provide a workplace that ensures all employees can flourish and experience optimal mental health.

As a mindset and wellbeing coach, I am passionate about helping you develop new habits to live your best life. My goal is to empower each person I coach to go for *great* and create the life they have been dreaming of, whether it be a health goal, to step outside their comfort zone to follow a passion or to help them identify additional tools that will allow them to thrive more easily in an area that is troubling them.

I am professionally trained to help you achieve personal and professional transformation. The art of life coaching focuses on current and future possibilities, not past mistakes. It's about unlocking your potential to maximise your opportunities, performance, skills, attitude and relationships so that you can identify tangible ways to move forward.

I understand the challenge of changing course and the level of support that is needed in order to find the confidence to back yourself and own your choices. I also know that it is possible to break free from those patterns and now I've made it my mission to help you do the same. Through coaching, I will support you to establish options for real change, allowing you to get unstuck and balance the areas of your life that are meaningful to you.

I am so grateful that I get to do this each and every day and help people like you. I am in my happy place when I sit beside my clients and listen to what makes them who they are, what isn't gelling and what they want out of life moving forward. If you're ready to go for great, I'm excited to meet and work with you as your mindset and wellbeing coach.

Website: consciouslivinghub.com.au
Mobile: 0468 374 560
Email: ange@consciouslivinghub.com.au
Instagram: @consciouslivinghub
Facebook: consciouslivinghub

WHEN FINDING OUT ROCK BOTTOM HAS A BASEMENT, THE ONLY WAY IS UP

Anueta Madison-Vanderbuilt

For my twenty-eighth birthday, I received a spray tan kit from a business that was closing down. This would become a passionate hobby that turned me into the director of a company. I was born in Russia to Russian parents, so the harsh Australian sun burnt my pale white skin, and with my family's history of skin cancer, I decided early on that spray tans would just become part of my lifestyle.

After getting the kit, I began researching what went into spray tan solutions, as I didn't want it to be something I passively used without knowing more about it. I wanted to have the best knowledge, service and products as a point of difference. I taught my husband how to spray tan me so I could always be bronze and be the poster board for my business. My full-time job was a stay-at-home mum. I had three young kids, two boys and a baby girl, who I was with twenty-four seven.

After the word spread about my high-quality spray tans, I had new clients booking in weekly. We couldn't afford a babysitter, so I had to work smarter not harder. I took a risk and made my business hours 6pm–midnight, and I honestly believe that was a key part in my success over the years. Working after business hours, other mums were able to have their partner be with their kids so they could come and get a spray tan, or I would come to them; a mobile, after-hours beauty service was something no-one else was offering. My saying goes, 'I work the hours others won't to live the life that others don't.' Finding a product or service that creates a solution is a greatest business hack.

To add to the chaos, I was also finishing my psychology degree. I had started it a couple years before, but with each new baby being born, I deferred for a semester, and so it took longer than anticipated. Still, I was very proud of myself for continuing my studies whilst working on my new business and raising three small kids.

We took a hit when my husband quit his job. He wasn't happy, and I wanted to support him in finding a more fulfilling career. This meant we went from a six-figure income to just above minimum wage, with five mouths to feed. Before I met my husband I was always financially independent, I moved out of home at seventeen and always had a budget and great relationship with money. I didn't want us to struggle financially, and as we had a spare bedroom, I looked into an au pair so I could work a little more during the day to help provide for our family. An au pair is a live-in international student who provides child care for a set number of hours per week in exchange for living expenses such as rent, bills and food. We found an amazing law student from Peru. Honestly, she saved my mental health during that period of my life. It's okay to outsource when you have to; asking for help isn't a weakness, it takes courage.

At the time, I worked three casual jobs: a sales assistant at a women's clothing store, a disability support worker and packing orders for an online kids clothing boutique, all while growing my spray tan business. It was all a bit of a blur!

An average day for me looked like:
- Getting up early with my kids.
- Making breakfast for my eldest.

- Breastfeeding the younger two and getting them in the pram for the walk to school.
- Putting the younger ones down to nap.
- Eating the crumbs out of my cleavage from breakfast and hurriedly trying to shower to get ready for work.
- At 11:30am our au pair would come out of her room after studying and take over with the younger two kids – feeding them lunch, putting them down for naps and playing with them.
- I would work at the clothing store from 12pm-9pm. (I'd have a half-hour break in the afternoon/early evening to drive home and breastfeed the younger two.)
- Return to the store and close at 9pm.
- Drive to my spray tan clients for late evening appointments.
- Arrive home early hours of the morning to study.

Despite having three casual jobs, I was not giving up my passion. I would spray tan from 9:30pm–1am most Thursdays. And yes, surprisingly, many people were happy with a tan at that time, in their own home, after their families were asleep and all the chores of the house had been done. Then they could unwind and relax in their tan in the privacy of their own home and just rinse an hour or so later.

I could feel the burnout coming on; I was pouring from an empty cup, but my life was about to get much harder.

It was approximately 9pm one night and all three kids were asleep. My husband was in the shower and I was sitting in bed having my first rest for the day, scrolling through Instagram on my phone. It was then that I received the phone call that changed my life forever.

A friend of mine asked if she could call me, but 'only if my husband wasn't around'. She said, 'Do you know where your husband was today?' My stomach dropped. I knew, I just *knew* what this meant, but I still asked, 'What do you mean? He was at work all day.' My husband worked in real estate, which meant every Saturday was auction day. In fact, he had messaged me and called me about a lunch meeting he was having with a couple who was selling a home that day. My friend proceeded to tell me that she saw him at a restaurant she was having lunch at. She told me he was sitting with a woman and acting very flirtatious.

I knew exactly who it would be. I think every woman has an intuition where she just *knows* something isn't right. She was a new girl at the office. A young, nineteen-year-old woman, whose desk was next to my husband's. When I visited him at the office with the kids, I'd always make an effort to be nice to her.

I went straight into survival mode. I wasn't even angry or upset, I just knew what I had to do. I thanked my friend for telling me and hung up the call as my husband got out of the shower. I pretended nothing had happened, after all, it was his birthday the next day (he was thirty-six at the time), and I really didn't want to ruin that.

Two days later was Monday and I managed to get to the library – and so began my journey of leaving my marriage. I downloaded his phone bill to make sure I had all the evidence: six weeks' worth of text messages between them. I even confirmed with the manager of the restaurant that they were there. For my peace of mind I needed to be sure.

My next step was to prepare for my new life. I didn't even have a bank account and my name wasn't on the mortgage of the house, so I knew I had to protect myself. I found a family lawyer who would take payment after we had settled, and I filed for single parent pension through Centrelink, opening my first bank account in my own name in years.

I actually didn't exist on paper, and I had to prove who I was all over again. I applied to take out money from my superannuation, because my husband would inevitably close the bank accounts I had access to, as I was only a signatory.

I knew I needed to be able to provide for my kids until settlement, but I had no idea how hard things were about to get. When we split, I spent the next six months close to homelessness as he not only closed the bank accounts, but began selling the home whilst the kids and I were still in it. We used Salvos and Vinnies services to get food hampers for the kids and me to eat and have support in case the house sold before we found a rental.

I hit rock bottom. I had to put my pride aside and accept help from multiple social workers and government support services to keep us afloat. I distinctly remember standing in the line at my local Salvation Army food drop point with my three kids as I said, 'When I get back on my feet I will pay it forward and help other mothers in need.' I stayed true to that promise; twelve months later, thanks to the money I took out of my super, I was able to close on a commercial lease to open my own spray tan and teeth-whitening studio. I was able to pay for a full year of school fees and uniform fees for seven students at my son's school, one student from each year, prep to grade six, whose families were doing it tough.

Starting from scratch was hard but it meant I could write this new chapter any way I wanted. I could reinvent myself and try new things. I could fail again and again and it didn't matter because we were already at rock bottom. I had to find ways to survive and not lose myself in the process.

Here's what I learnt very quickly: I'm not that mum. This has been the biggest help in reducing my risk of burnout. I'm not a morning person; getting up early to make their breakfast used to mean I would be a cranky mum before 9am even hit. Breakfast is the meal they have to make themselves. It not only makes them more independent, it teaches them to help their siblings and show care, but it also means we start the day off on the right foot and I'm not raising young men who rely on the women in their family to spoonfeed them. I get up, give them cuddles and get ready in my bathroom where I have some alone time. They have learnt about consent, and if the door is shut it means I'm changing and they don't have consent to open the door and see my body unless it's an emergency. This teaches them patience and I'm not hurriedly getting ready ending up starting the day frustrated.

It's about learning what works for you and what your strengths and weaknesses are. And mornings are definitely my weakness! We all get to start our day productively, calmly and without any resentment or frustration. This took some time to instil, but after a couple of months it became second nature and my eldest even asked his dad to have a similar routine for when they stay at his house.

Fast-forward a couple of years and I can wake up at 8am, lay in bed and then calmly get dressed for the gym while the kids all make their own breakfast. I come downstairs fresh and ready at 8:30am to a clean kitchen, wrappers are in the bin and bowls in the dishwasher – I just have to drive them to school. I've made lunches the night before with their help so there's no excuse that they won't eat what's in their lunch box.

Food – this was another battle I chose to retire from! Whether they want two snacks or ten different food varieties, I let them pick. Demanding they eat all their lunch or dinner that *I'd* chosen ended in arguments and an unhealthy relationship with food. We all have days when we don't feel like eating certain things or different quantities of food, so by asking them to choose what goes into their lunch or dinner means they'll mostly eat it all. I give them options of healthy food and snacks when we are grocery shopping at the start of the week so it eliminates unnecessary arguments later. They feel they are part of the process and have a say as to what goes into their bodies.

I've applied this mindset to a few other mum obligations. I hate baking, it gives me anxiety; the mess, the eggs, the dust from the flour – I just cant. So I'm not *that mum*. They bake with their nonna or my best friend when she comes over. Hand-making slime; I'm not that mum! Painting in the house; I'm not that mum. Braiding my daughters hair; I'm not that mum. I've stopped matching their socks and underwear and putting them in separate draws. They all have similar sizes, so now I just throw them in the sock box and they pick two every morning and go with it. If you're particular about having everything ironed or folded and matched, then this isn't for you, but if doing the laundry overwhelms you, pick and choose what is a priority. My kids have four pull-out boxes in each of their wardrobes. Tops, PJs, shorts/skirts and pants. Just four categories represent all their clothing and I just throw it in by size. There's no spending time folding everything nicely when they would just get dirty and wrinkled within minutes of wear. I decided it wasn't important to me and I'm not that mum. If unloading the washer or drier is too much on a certain day, just put it on to wash again and unload when you have the strength to tackle that. If unloading the dishwasher is too much today, put it on a second wash. The amount it costs in water and to run those machines is miniscule in comparison to the cost to your mental health.

I won't be ashamed of *not being that mum*. I know my strengths and weaknesses, and I do the things I know I'm good at and enjoy with my kids. They feel the love and passion so much more. I AM the mum who will go on the playground in the play centre and be a big kid in the tunnels and slides. I AM the mum who will rock climb, and oh my goodness do they love it. I'm the mum that teaches them about diverse cultures and religions and backgrounds and pronouns and sexuality and genders, or lack thereof, and the LGBTQIA+ community. I'm the mum who will be so excited for my sons to play with cars and wear a skirt and nail polish at the same time. I'm the mum who will stay up late teaching them positive affirmations and discussing what anxiety feels like in their bellies and make them feel loved and heard and acknowledged. I'll ride their little scooter for hours and chase them and do cartwheels all day – I'm that mum. I now have the capacity to do that more often and it doesn't add to my anxiety or possibility of burnout. You can be whatever mum, woman, person you choose to be – whatever makes you happy. Don't allow the world of Pinterest and perfect Instagram families trick you. No-one has their shit together, no-one is perfect all of the time and we all say 'fuck them kids' under our breath every now and then.

And that's okay.

ANUETA MADISON-VANDERBUILT

Anueta was born in Odessa, Ukraine, in 1990 and her family fled the country when she was just six months old. She moved with her parents to Tel Aviv, Israel, and experienced her early years surrounded by family and laughter. Hebrew was her first language, followed closely by Russian. At five years old, her family moved again, this time to Melbourne, Australia. She started primary school months after arriving and picked up English quickly, becoming the interpreter for the family. Her younger years were shrouded in physical abuse at the hands of her father for which she had to have reconstructive facial surgery years later.

Finally, her parents divorced, and at the age of seven, she became her mother's carer when she discovered she had terminal cancer. They spent the next six months in and out of hospital until they received the amazing news that, by some miracle, her mother was in remission.

Her maternal grandparents arrived in Australia and began to help her mother through recovery, but Anueta's childhood would be lost forever.

Anueta's mother met the man who would become her stepfather when she was ten years old; he was an international student from Pakistan, and with their clashing religion – her family being Jewish and his being Muslim – they had to fight bigotry and racism in their community and bullying at Anueta's school.

Anueta's home life took a dark turn as her stepfather started grooming her shortly after he married her mother which lead to him sexually abusing her for the next five years. Anueta fought mental health issues during this time as she didn't tell anyone, thinking she wouldn't be believed. At the age of sixteen she attempted suicide three times, and upon her mother finding out, she was sent to complete year twelve in America.

Anueta had an amazing experience in Texas and her host family are still very much a part of her life to this day. Upon her return, Anueta moved out of home and ended her relationship with her family just after turning eighteen years old. By age twenty, she earned a Diploma in Creative Industries, was financially stable and had a great home of her own. She felt ready to start a family and had her first son Roman four days before her twenty-first birthday.

She wanted family of her own so badly, but unfortunately it wasn't to last long as the father of her child became aggressive and violent towards both her and their infant. Anueta knew she had to end the cycle of domestic violence and left when her son was just a couple of months old. Again, she started over on her own as a single mother.

Eight months later, she met the man who would become her husband, and together with his Italian family, they created a life and a home. Anueta had her rainbow baby boy at twenty-six years old after a miscarriage two years prior, and fifteen months later she had her baby girl. She quit her fifteen-year career in retail and became a stay-at-home mum, only pursuing her hobby of spray tanning on the side and working casually to help support her family many years later.

After eight years together and six years of marriage, Anueta found herself starting over again as a single mum of three facing homelessness with zero dollars to her name.

Anueta has now turned that spray tan hobby into a company with staff and runs multiple online businesses. She has set up a support fund at her son's school which pays for the yearly school and uniform fees of seven children per year and she also volunteers at the school. She has completed a Bachelor of Social Science majoring in behavioural studies and is currently undertaking a certificate in early education.

Anueta and her three children live in Melbourne's north with their dog Jax. Her definition of success is giving her children the childhood she never had and helping other women and children find a voice and a right to feel safe and acknowledged.

DO WHAT MAKES YOU HAPPY

Bee Lim

'Because I knew you …
I have been changed for good.'
'For Good' – Idina Menzel & Kristin Chenoweth

10 June 2021 marked the start of one of the darkest periods in my life.

The doctor said, 'Your pa has terminal cancer.' I remember my mother mumbling these words to me in our native Teochew dialect, the blood draining from her face. Working as a psycho-oncology therapist, I have seen many cancer patients and carers in my consulting room. Their faces and stories flashed through my mind, stopping abruptly on my father, the man I have always associated with gallantry and invincibility.

The months following Pa's diagnosis became a blur. Earlier that year, we had hoped my parents would start their retirement in Australia. I was instead having to apply for travel exemptions to leave the country so I could be home to support my father with his cancer treatment. This also meant leaving my husband and young son behind for the foreseeable future. *As long as it takes for Pa to get better*, I thought.

All my life, I had been a classic overachiever who lived to exceed expectations. I dreamt of becoming a therapist and running my own therapy practice, even when my family opposed it. A friend often reminds me that I woke up from a coma, caused by an autoimmune disease, and two days later completed a national admission exam in a small, poorly lit hospital room. During my father's diagnosis, I was overwhelmed and exhausted. In addition to seeing clients and managing my private practice, my new routine became attending and translating at oncology appointments, staying vigilant of potential drug interaction effects and keeping the family's hopes alive. At the same time, I tried to stay present with my husband and toddler, feeling deeply guilty at my physical absence. I was constantly worried I wasn't doing enough for my family and clients.

If I had been a client walking into my consulting room, I would have immediately seen the persona susceptible to burnout: a perfectionistic overcompensator with a strong guilt-inducing inner critic. There are many reasons we repeatedly strive for perfection – fear of disapproval of others and fear that we are not good enough (never enough), which substantiates our story of failure. The most damaging aspect of perfectionism is not the setting of high standards, but the belief that failing to meet those standards confirms we are defective and worthless. You would hardly be surprised to know that my father ran his business from the hospital bed, even when he had an IV administering chemotherapy inserted into his arm.

What about the voice that tells us we are selfish to put our needs first, and that others cannot *ever* be let down? 'Human givers', a concept coined by philosopher Kate Manne, expect themselves to put all their energy into supporting others' success and providing comfort. They must be pleasing, happy, calm, generous and available to meet the needs of others at all times. When we strive to meet such excessively high internalised standards and negate our own needs for nurturance and rest, we burnout.

I have learned a lot from my personal experience of busyness and exhaustion, as well as working with clients to recover from their burnouts to live a more balanced, aligned life. From a place of continued restoration, I learned to slow down and be kind to myself by reacquainting myself with my inner child, challenging my inner critic, setting boundaries with toxic others and finding joy again through intentional play.

ATTUNING TO VULNERABILITY: REACQUAINTING YOURSELF WITH YOUR INNER CHILD

Once, during the Lunar New Year festivities, my father shared stories from his early childhood. He had lost his mother when he was twelve. As the eldest, he dropped out of school to financially support his four younger siblings, with no help from his affluent extended family. At his wake, more stories were shared about his deprived, impoverished younger years: sleeping on flattened cardboard boxes night after night or waking up in the small hours to work multiple jobs to earn a living. These vulnerable impressions of my father were jarring next to the image of him I'd had my whole life. His tough facade was the result of his survival mechanism, his scars swallowing the bitterness of life.

When my father was confronted with his mortality, I avoided checking in with myself. I feared becoming an emotional blob that would render me useless and burdensome. Family and close friends hesitated to ask how he was (we were) doing, and we kept avoiding the painful subject, the elephant in the room. 'He never once mentioned death,' my mother repeated to many at the wake. *He never once mentioned pain*, I thought, sitting with him through hours of chemotherapy. Throughout his life, my father had modelled for me incredible strength, but he did not show me vulnerability or how to lean on others for emotional support.

Even when vulnerability has become such a buzzword in our culture, it takes immense courage, gentleness and persistence to see and sit with our vulnerability. So many of us are afraid of what we will find if we attune to the vulnerable parts. *A sad child shutting down in a dark corner? A young one shouting at the top of their lungs, demanding attention? Or an anxious kid who is unsure whether to approach or retreat?* And do we have time for this vulnerable part when we are already so drained, running after others and providing what they need?

Recognising and accepting that our needs are worthy of being met begins with treating ourselves as our own beloved, someone we love with our whole heart. The following script is one I use frequently, and also with my clients, to help the fearful, vulnerable part of us feel seen and heard. For this exercise, you might want to get a picture of yourself as a child to encourage you to connect with the little you.

Close your eyes and connect with the child part of you. Ask the child where they want to be, where they feel the safest. Imagine taking the little you to this space. Find a comfortable place to sit and put the little you on your lap. Talk to them about what they need now. It could be they need you to check in more often; perhaps you feel detached, and your inner child is the last thing you consider. Ask, check in and find out what this young part of you needs to feel less afraid – and provide it. Comfort and reassure the little you. You can't get rid of your painful experiences, but you can be reassuring and listen to the fears and concerns that the young part of you has. Make a commitment to them that you will regularly check in. That you won't ignore their fears or needs. The little child part of you is precious and deserves love, protection and fun.

At first, the tuning into our vulnerability will feel strange. Our inner child could even be hidden under layers upon layers of defenses, like it was for my father and his hard facade. Trust in the process and stick with it. We have years of practise of neglecting and rejecting our core needs. This exercise offers us an accessible way to attune, listen and heal.

WORKAHOLISM, SLOWING DOWN AND SAYING NO: CHALLENGING YOUR INNER CRITIC & SETTING BOUNDARIES WITH TOXIC OTHERS

My father was a workaholic. 'He'll only stop working the day he lies flat-bottomed,' my uncle remarked about my father many years ago.

Sadly, my uncle's words came to pass as prophecy. Growing up in poverty, my father understood the pain of deprivation. To cope, he learned to hustle and work excessively long hours without griping about his seven-day work schedule.

My father taught me to be industrious and dedicated, but he did not teach me to slow down and set boundaries for my health. A thirty-two-year longitudinal study[1] shows that prolonged working hours increase the risk for heart disease, cancer, arthritis and diabetes, especially in women. *Karoshi*, a Japanese word, literally translates to 'death by overwork' and embodies the sentiment. We overwork to appease perfectionism, the demanding inner critic who urges us to work more – or just do more – so that we can be worthy and loved.

Breaking free from your inner critic

Our family and cultural upbringing shape our inner critic. Research by Dr Bryan Robinson, an expert in workaholism, shows that adult children with a workaholic parent carry invisible psychological scars. From the outside, these children often grow into enviable, high-functioning adults who are responsible, performance oriented and in control of situations. Inside, however, they feel they are never enough and mercilessly adhere to an unattainable standard of perfection.

Many of us have an unhealthy attachment to our critic, despite its hurtful and immobilising impact. This critical inner voice urges us to work extra hard so we can be enough, but also takes away from us being able to let go, have fun and be creative. Think of the immense costs of attaching to our inner critic and being consumed by feelings of fear and unworthiness: the ideas unshared, the creativity unexpressed, the talents unused and the lives unlived, all because our critic refuses our needs to explore, experiment and learn curiously. Still, we wonder if we want to

1 Allard E Dembe and Xiaoxi Yao, 'Chronic Disease Risks from Exposure to Long-Hour Work Schedules Over a 32-Year Period,' *Journal of Occupational and Environmental Medicine,* 58, no 9 (2016): 861-867 pubmed.ncbi.nlm.nih.gov/27305843

silence our inner critic: *I'll fall apart without my critic motivating me, I am no-one without my critic.* We are so used to living with this voice that it is difficult to imagine a healthier, kinder alternative.

Our early life experiences sowed the seeds and laid down patterns for our future relationships. If we do not understand them, we cannot develop new, healthier habits, and the negative cycle persists. Understanding the origin of our inner critic and labelling the critic's voice is the first step to unhooking from its grip. One simple way is to point out: *I see what you are doing, critic [or any name you have given the critic]. Back off.* This dampens the critic's rigid control and our unhealthy attachment to it. Moreover, there is no scientific evidence suggesting that submitting to our inner critic will move us towards our goals.

Setting boundaries without guilt

Not only do we need to name and resist our inner critic, we also need to recognise and distance ourselves from the toxic others. 'You happy, I happy,' my father frequently said, and it speaks of his self-sacrificing nature and the great lengths he would go for others, even when he was sick and depleted. In his book, *Give and Take*, bestselling author Adam Grant would have classified my father as a selfless giver, someone who gives his time and energy regardless of his own needs. Selfless givers pay a price for their care for others. While selfless seems admirable, if we do not consider our own interests, we risk burning out and becoming resentful.

Our culture, religion and families condition us to put others first and our needs last. How often do we give up on our needs simply because it seemed more important to maintain peace or save face? When we notice troubled relationships in our lives, there is an impulse to avoid and turn a blind eye. We find it difficult to let go of toxic and draining relationships, especially when the one who consumes all our energy is a family member or close friend.

We need to name the flawed, dysfunctional dynamic so we can stop the energy leak. Whether the interaction pattern is enmeshed, dependent or abusive, commit yourself to changing the dance. We don't owe anyone anything; we do owe our inner child the courage to say no and protect them from social toxins that poison their wellness and safety. Boundaries offer us a way to honour and love ourselves, and others, well. When we set and uphold our boundaries, we communicate to others: *Yes, your needs matter, and mine too.*

SLOW DOWN AND FIND JOY THROUGH PLAY

'What's our plan for tomorrow?' 'Play, Mommy!'

'What are you doing?' 'Just watching the clouds.'

These are snippets of conversations between me and my four-year-old.

Our children are our best teachers for play. A child's play focuses simply on the enjoyment, not the result. When we are busy adulting, our need for spontaneity and play is often neglected. Many of us languish in states of burnout, anxiety and depression because of chronic deprivation of fun and play. We forget the happy freedom to be intensely absorbed in what we do – painting, writing, dancing, jumping on the trampoline, falling into a pile of leaves – that we completely lose track of time.

Dr Stuart Brown, psychiatrist and founder of the National Institute for Play, identifies eight distinct play personalities: the joker, the kinesthete, the explorer, the competitor, the director, the collector, the artist and the storyteller.[2] Reclaiming play as both a fun and meaningful practice helps us connect with the *happy child* part of ourselves and our purpose. Slowing down to play is the prerequisite for creative innovation and impactful work. An exercise that helps us to be more intentional

---

2 The eight play personalities: the joker who delights in comical play; the kinesthete who enjoys movements and physical play; the explorer who thrives on novelty and new experiences; the competitor who likes winning and being the best; the director who loves being in charge and watching their plans played out; the collector who loves curating and organising their collections, whether experiential or material; the creator who delights in creating and making things; and the storyteller who finds joy in unlocking stories and tapping into their imagination.

about our play is to take time and remember the activities we loved as a child, the experiences that brought laughter and smiles to our faces. These memories provide clues to access and honour play experiences that best express who we are as adults. And the next step: schedule time to play and play!

When I remember my father, the memories of him singing karaoke in the living room of our family home come back. Free. Animated. In a state of flow. Since his death, I have thought about what stories of him I would tell my son to keep the memories of his gong gong (grandfather) alive. In his life, my father taught me to be tough, to work hard and to love self-sacrificially. In his death, he taught me to be vulnerable, to slow down and to say no. Perhaps the legacy he left behind, rather than *you happy, I happy* is *do what makes you happy.*

BEE LIM

Bee Lim, PhD, is a clinical psychologist and the founder of a thriving private practice in Sydney, whose mission is to inspire hope and guide clients towards achieving wellness through integrative, evidence-based mental health care.

Bee completed her postdoctoral fellowships in psycho-oncology and positive psychology. Originally from Malaysia, she is fluent in Mandarin and a number of Asian dialects. She has consulted for the Cancer Council New South Wales on a three-year project developing in-language webinars and resources for cancer survivors and carers who face barriers accessing support in Australia. She has appeared on the SBS (Chinese) radio program, discussing the mental health challenges facing Chinese Australians. Bee's research has been published in *Psycho-oncology, The Journal of Positive Psychology, Medical Teacher* and more.

Bee lives in Sydney, Australia, with her husband and son. Together, they are working on their passion project on meaningful play.

NGALIMING WIRU DHADHADYABAYA

(OUR SPIRIT IS GETTING STRONGER)

Bianca F Stawiarski

As women we are constantly being told that we can have it all. We can be caring mothers, have careers or be in business, improve our education, be in a loving reciprocal romantic relationship, have strong friendships, manage a home and honour our family and community obligations. As First Nations women, the weight of this 'opportunity' is further compounded by the added internal and external pressures of walking in two worlds, with competing pressures and responsibilities. While we can do all these things, if we are brutally honest with each other, we'd likely say that this is rarely successful and certainly not balanced. Success in one of these areas of life often comes at a cost in other areas – either to us, our career, to those we love and care about or to our community. So why do we continue to place ourselves under this pressure?

I think part of the problem is that when we become really busy, when we're peddling as fast as we can and just not getting anywhere, we think that the only way out of the situation is to work harder, be a better mum, try harder at that relationship … if we just persevere a little longer, then we can take a break. Then we will have balance. Then we can have a holiday or spend more time with our children. But do you know what happens? Firstly, a bearing comes loose, then a cog falls out (a relationship fails), or a wheel falls off (you burnout), and *everything* grinds to a halt. All those things that were so important are now less so. While this chapter is not about burnout, it IS about recognising and finding balance and connection, so that *ngaliming wiru dhadhadyabaya* (our spirit is getting stronger).

WINDHU NGARDI YUWA-YUWAGA
(THE WIND IS BLOWING STRONG)

Anyone who knows me knows I resonate with strong cleansing ancestral winds. They ground me and remind me of who I am and what is important. Maybe it's the *warida* (wedge-tailed eagle) in me that loves the wind, but in the last seven years, it's been more like flying through a cyclone. In that time, I retired from over two decades of working for the commonwealth government, experienced a marriage breakdown, survived a devastating bushfire and became a single parent with no job at the age of forty-two. I then decided to study and start my own business so I could focus on my children. Writing this now, looking back, it really was one of my least thought-out ideas! In the seven years since late 2015, I launched a successful international Indigenous social enterprise focusing on mental health from a decolonised perspective, particularly working with clients who have experienced complex trauma. I also gained life coaching, equine-assisted psychotherapy and counselling qualifications and am now undertaking a PhD in my 'spare' time (of which there really isn't any). I also had another failed significant relationship, finding myself soaring solo again. I worked seven days a week for over four years straight trying to get ahead, telling myself that, *I will rest when I reach a level that can adequately support my family.* Whilst I was making headway, I was isolating myself from my friends, family and community, but most importantly, I wasn't always there for my children. From the outside I looked successful, but at what cost? It is with this in mind that leads me to my first suggestion:

Acknowledge where you are right now.

This is, in effect, doing an awareness audit of your life. It requires extreme bravery and honesty to look at your life without a lens and to recognise your rawness, pain and grief. Only through this process can you have any hope of creating change. It embraces the theory of paradoxical change, where 'change occurs when one becomes what he is, not when he tries to become what he is not'.[1] Awareness gives us choice – even if this process is confronting. Awareness requires us to sit still and listen deeply – within our bodies, mind and spirit, in our connection with Country and Ancestors. What do you hear? What do you see and feel? This is beyond the physical aspect of the senses. This is deeply sitting in ceremony with ourselves, Country and Ancestors – recognising and listening for the answers. Do you have the courage to truly look at your life away from the pressures of societal or community expectations? It's not something we usually ask ourselves – *Do I have the courage?* It does get easier over time, but when first starting out it can be downright scary!

GABI WIDAWU WARANGGUWA (THE RAIN IS FALLING SLOWLY)

Slow-falling rain encourages us to pause, reflect and see the world differently. This brings balance, is cleansing and connecting. Interestingly, most people would describe rain as an external sensation, but what if you truly saw the rain touching not only your skin, hair and clothes, but also cleansing and energising your spirit too! In effect, letting the tiredness wash away, leaving you fresh, sparkling and renewed.

While I am absolutely energised and passionate about what I do, it was obvious that my working pace and high productivity wasn't sustainable long-term. It was the reminders from my partner at the time, to take

---

1 Beisser 1970: 77

time for me, my family and friendships that encouraged me to incorporate a day off a week – embracing the rain, Country and my connection. It is also worth noting that, to be honest, as a mental health therapist and coach, I needed to continue to do my own healing so that I could hold space for others. Working outside in a decolonised approach to healing meant I was constantly being resourced and connected to Country, as well as moving my body in a form of ceremony. While I believe this connection has insulated me from burnout, I still needed to focus on more balance in my life. I had to make some difficult but necessary decisions which required yet another pivot in my business. This meant that I needed to reduce my individual client days in preference for other services that enabled an impact on a larger group of people with a reduced time commitment. This increased my available time for my family, my personal and community relationships, my reflection time and me. Although I can still improve this balance further, I acknowledge that this is a starting point with short- and long-term plans to further improve this. Aunty Miriam-Rose Ungunmerr Bauman explains the importance of being, knowing and doing from a First Nations perspective in a powerful way:

Dadirri recognises the deep spring that is inside us. We call on it and it calls on us ... When I experience dadirri, I am made whole again. I can sit on the riverbank or walk through the trees, even if someone close to me has passed away, I can find my peace in this silent awareness. There is no need for words ... The contemplative way of dadirri spreads over our whole life. It renews us and brings us peace. It makes us feel whole again.[2]

Just reading her words is like a soothing balm of bush medicine rubbed onto an aching muscle, or a cool breeze on a warm summer's day. Understanding the need to become still with deep inner reflection, is my second suggestion.

---

2 Ungunmerr Bauman 1988: pp1-2

Prioritise and implement an approach involving stillness and deep inner listening while in connection with Country

If we continue to be focused on being 'busy' with little or no time for recharging our batteries, connecting to Country or spending time enriching our families and communities, we will continue to be pulled in multiple directions, eventually growing to resent our lives. This leads to further disconnection from our families and communities. We honour no-one, and certainly not ourselves, by sitting within that energy. It is also worth recognising that this hectic working pace – an addiction of sorts – may be another way to avoid looking at our inner world and truly seeing the things that we are trying so hard to avoid. If you explored this, what would you discover is the truth telling for you?

NGALIMING MABARN (OUR MEDICINE)

One of my absolute favourite quotes is from an American First Nation's oral tradition, and you can probably guess why I love this so much:

> *'The medicine is already within the pain and suffering. You just have to look deeply and quietly. Then you realise that it has been there the whole time.'*
> ***Saying from American First Nation's oral tradition***
> ***(cited in Hubl 2020: xv)***

Hearing or reading those words is like a call to action for each and every one of us. Each of us INNATELY knows how to heal, how to include balance into our lives, to slow down and 'un-busy' ourselves, reducing our stress levels and also recognising when we are being incongruent with how we feel. If we know this innately, then why do we continue to hear alarming statistics such as burnout being listed as a growing global crisis or absenteeism/presenteeism costing businesses in each country tens of billions of dollars in lost productivity each year? Why do we continue to work ourselves into dysregulated bodies, high blood pressure, high stress levels and isolation from others, where we are living on caffeine to function and using increasing amounts of alcohol to slow down the hamster wheel of busy? Too often, when people first come to work with me, they consistently share their stories of abdicating their healing journey to a 'professional' because they feel pressured to do that. It is a common story where the therapist takes on the role of 'expert' rather than acknowledging the expertise that each person contains within themselves.

Let me be very clear ... YOU KNOW WHAT YOU NEED. You always have. Please note, though, healing and balance, and how they are perceived, can be very different for all of us. Each of us are unique and diverse, so the way we de-stress our lives also needs to be. If we look at balance, healing and connection through a decolonised lens, we realise that Indigenous healing practices and approaches – which have been practiced for millennia – are integral to improving our mental health and wellbeing, as well as reducing our levels of stress. Indigenous healing practices support both First Nations and non-Indigenous peoples to move back into connection, health and balance. They are 'effective in altering neural systems in the stress response in both animal models and humans'.[3] Importantly, these are no longer considered as lacking evidence-based practices. The interesting part is that this is not something that can be learned in books or held at arm's length, it must be felt in all its rawness, as a somatosensory experience in connection with others and Country, not in isolation. Despite what Western medicine has determined is healing, Perry (2008) explores what Indigenous healing practices may look like and how they improve our health:

The most remarkable quality of these elements is that together they create a total neurobiological experience influencing cortical, limbic, diencephalic and brainstem systems (not unlike the pervasive neurobiological impact of trauma):

* *Retell the story.*

---

3 Perry, cited in Malchiodi 2015: xii

- *Hold each other.*
- *Massage, dance, sing.*
- *Create images of the battle, hunt and death.*
- *Fill literature, sculpture and drama with retellings.*
- *Reconnect to loved ones and community.*
- *Celebrate, eat and share.*

These Aboriginal healing practices are repetitive, rhythmic, relevant, relational, respectful and rewarding … These practices emerged because they worked. People felt better and functioned better.[4]

What does this all mean? Quite simply, that we don't need a mental health qualification to heal ourselves, to find balance or to look within and remember the joy of life. We do, however, need safe connections with others, and it can help having someone to support you on your journey – whether that be a therapist, coach, mentor, partner or friend. It is through connection with each other, with touch, with the simple sharing of food, of song, of dance, that we can remember who we are. We have tens of thousands of years of evidence from First Nations peoples around the world that show that these approaches work.

Ask yourself what you need so that you can incorporate balance into your life. Have you ever allowed yourself to ask that question or spent the time in quiet reflection to hear the answer? For example, does your body need to move, dance, swim or walk? Do you need to incorporate a form of ceremony into your life, honouring the start and end of each day? What is it that you want to achieve, and what is less important? What can you stop doing? What can you delegate? For myself, having an amazing lady (biggest shout-out to the gorgeous Sue) coming in to clean my house every week reduced my feelings of guilt, allowed me to breathe, and importantly, I was able to focus on things that were more important but still enjoy a beautifully clean house. This made such a huge difference to my life and my family's life.

---

4 Perry, cited in Malchiodi 2015: xi–xii

Reflecting on all we have explored and yarned about throughout this chapter, I'd like to issue you with a challenge! This challenge isn't going to be soft and fluffy with neatly packaged edges. It's going to be confronting, raw and difficult. You likely may not want to listen, but my challenge is to be open to the possibilities. Be honest about where you are right now and what YOU really need. Notice I said YOU. This is not what others think you need. Being honest about this isn't going to make you popular, but it does make you authentic and congruent. Also, it's probably a fairly safe assumption that as you are reading this book it likely means that life isn't quite where you'd like it to be. So, I ask you, where do you imagine your life to be? Even for a moment, can you feel what life would look like with restorative, enriching balance? Can you see, feel and breathe this new and resourceful existence and then finally step through that door? I'd like to leave you with a poem, it is up to you what meaning you take from this.

The Door
Jessie Belle Rittenhouse (1918)

There was a door stood long ajar
That one had left for me,
While I went trying other doors
To which I had no key.

And when at last I turned to seek
The refuge and the light,
A gust of wind had shut the door
And left me in the night"

Let this writing be your reminder of the door that is waiting for you.

BIANCA F STAWIARSKI

Bianca Stawiarski is the founder and managing director of Warida Wholistic Wellness. She is a strong Badimaya and Ukrainian woman, who is a centred and purpose-driven healer, consultant, coach, speaker, lecturer, bestselling and international author, trainer and change-maker.

Bianca infuses her calming, resilient, earthy, Indigenous connectedness into all that she does. As well as the work she does on Country, Bianca is sought out by organisations, companies and publications from across the globe. She is a certified mental health practitioner with an interest in supporting people who have experienced complex trauma, bringing the therapeutic space outside of four walls. She holds a master's in counselling practice, a diploma of life coaching, postgrad diploma of counselling, certificate in equine-assisted psychotherapy, a bachelor of Aboriginal studies and a diploma of contracting (government), amongst other qualifications. She is also currently undertaking a PhD exploring whether the Indigenous healing practice of dadirri can assist people with dissociative identity disorder create inner communities of care. Bianca hopes that the results can benefit some of our world's most disadvantaged and vulnerable people and provide a platform for people with lived experience to have their voices heard.

Bianca founded Warida Wholistic Wellness by recognising that communities needed something different to Western clinical approaches to improve the growing mental health crisis around the world. She combined a clinical and relational approach of Indigenous healing practices together, outside on Country, facilitating a unique approach to healing needed in our communities. Whether that be working with Warida's horses through equine-assisted psychotherapy, taking a walk on Country with bush therapy, yarning circles or drawing upon the natural wisdom of the grandmother tree, Bianca works in an intuitive and integrative decolonised therapeutic approach. She is also a strong advocate for women in business and Indigenous businesses, volunteering her time to help them succeed. Warida Wholistic Wellness is Supply Nation certified and Social Traders certified Indigenous social enterprise operating at an international level.

Her work has been recognised over the years, with one recognition of note winning the 2021 Global Business Mothers Awards in the Women Will Change the World and Oceania Business Excellence categories. This has encouraged her to reach further afield, providing online services in transformational coaching, therapy, business support and personal development so that women have access to holistic specialist support regardless of where they live.

Bianca lives on Kaurna Country with her two amazing adult children Savannah and Orson, her father Nick and a menagerie of four-legged family. In her spare time, Bianca competes internationally in horse archery.

Website: warida.com.au

MINDFULNESS MATTERS

Chantal Burling

I was eight years old and I was convinced that *this* was the night I was going to die.

It was the first time I had ever had a panic attack. I'd never experienced anything like it before, and I was absolutely terrified. My parents tried their best to console me, but this wasn't something they'd ever dealt with before either. They told me I was okay and that everything was going to be fine. And eventually, I fell asleep.

I don't remember talking to them about it again. That was the way it was back then. No-one talked about mental health. Nearly twenty years on, and I had become accustomed to a feeling of overwhelm and anxiety. I started to believe it was normal and that everyone felt that way.

When my first child was born, I knew there would be an adjustment period, and I had come to terms with sleep deprivation. What I hadn't expected was the almost constant checking to make sure he was still breathing or the panic about being left on my own all day with a newborn.

I put it down to the nerves of being a new mum and moved on as best as I could. Things got worse, and I started to isolate myself; I never left the house. The only people I interacted with were my husband and my parents when they came to visit. The stress was taking its toll, and burnout was becoming a real problem.

I finally began to realise something was seriously wrong when my son was about nine months old. I was home alone with the baby. He was teething so he'd spent most of the day fussing and crying – and I lost it. I put him on his play mat, sat down on the couch and cried. I felt like a failure. I was exhausted and scared, feeling completely out of my depth.

When I was finally able to pull myself together, I cradled my son and spent the next few hours researching why I felt the way I did. I felt ashamed and embarrassed when I realised that I might be suffering from anxiety, depression and burnout.

Why were my body and my brain betraying me? Why was I not strong enough to cope when so many others seemed to manage just fine?

It took a few months and more breakdowns before I finally found the strength to seek help. I felt hopeless and that no-one would understand, or even care.

My mental health and my busyness had robbed me of moments I can never get back. I was more worried about my son hurting himself than the magic of him taking his first steps. I was so preoccupied with making sure the house was clean, I forgot to sit down and play with my son or watch him find joy in the way a ball moves. I didn't want to live that way anymore. I spoke to my doctor who assured me that everything would be okay and that I was not alone.

And so began the hardest, most challenging time in my life.

I found a beautiful therapist and began seeing her every fortnight. I looked forward to our sessions and felt a wave of relief every time I sat down on her couch. It gave me a chance to speak without shame or fear of judgement. I spoke about things I'd held back. Things I'd always wanted to say but never had the courage. These appointments were a lifeline and I am so grateful for them. She led me down the path of mindfulness and encouraged alternate therapies that may be helpful to me as well. I discovered reiki, meditation and positive affirmations.

Reiki was one of the first alternate therapies I tried. I'd had some experience with it in the past, when a friend's mum performed reiki on my knee after I'd hurt it. It had helped ease my pain back then, and I was hopeful it would be able to help me now.

I found a practitioner close by and started seeing her monthly. In that hour every month, I learned how to make time for myself. To switch off and focus on me. It was here that I reclaimed some of myself back. I no longer saw myself as 'just a mum'.

Alongside reiki, I also started learning about meditation, and at first, I really struggled with learning how to sit and just 'be'. My thoughts would wander and I'd get distracted by all the things I *should* be doing instead. The dishes needed to be put in the dishwasher, the clothes needed hanging out, the floor needed vacuuming. The list seemed endless.

I started off slowly, with quick, five-minute meditations between nappy changes, working my way up incrementally until eventually getting to an hour. Even in those early days of five-minute meditations, I could feel the difference in my mood. I felt more grounded and calm, and when things became overwhelming, I would focus on my breath and meditate.

The housework could wait; it was going to get done eventually. In that moment in time, my focus was on me and my mental health, and that was more important than the floor getting vacuumed.

I also found the introduction of positive affirmations helped to improve my mood. I had become so judgemental of myself and believed I was not a good enough mother or wife. I believed I was not doing enough.

Positive affirmations helped to change the way I viewed my world. I became more positive, showing gratitude for the good things in my life. By repeating positive affirmations to myself, I started to trust and believe in myself again. I saw my strength, how ferociously I loved and how caring I could be. All the things I had forgotten or doubted.

Mindfulness was my biggest teacher. It showed me how to love my life, how to slow down and enjoy things, how to appreciate the smell of a flower, the beautiful sunset, the birdsong – all the little things that bring joy. These were things I had forgotten to notice because I was so caught up in my head and being busy.

Through my journey of healing my mental health, I began to rediscover who I am and what kind of person I wanted to be. I no longer wanted to live in fear. I wanted to be brave and let the people closest to me know when I was struggling. I wanted to have the courage to ask them for help when I needed it.

I no longer wanted to hide behind the walls I had built; walls that I thought were protecting me but were actually holding me back from being my authentic self and living my best life. I had been living a half-life, but now I was fully awake. I wanted to experience all the emotions, the good, the bad and the ecstatic. I'd been missing out on what it meant to be alive.

I had lost my passion for life. I'd become stuck in my busyness and anxiety. I lived minute by minute, hoping to get through the day with as few panic attacks as possible. I would wake up in the morning and my first thought would be to panic about the panic attack that would no doubt be happening soon. I would count down the hours until my husband got home, or I would escape to my mother-in-law's house for hours, just so I would have someone else around if I had a panic attack. I was wishing my days away. I couldn't remember the last time I laughed. I had shut myself off so completely because I was afraid of what might happen if I let myself 'feel'.

From the moment I started opening up about my struggles and

practicing mindfulness, my life started to become so much more full. I was more present in the moment. I played with the kids and we went on adventures and picnics. We stopped to watch ants and smell the flowers and watch the clouds float by.

Life became lighter.

I still struggled with moments of anxiety and depression but they were fewer. I was able to better manage these episodes and come out more quickly on the other side. I was able to put into practice all of my positive affirmations and mindfulness to get me through those moments.

The panic attacks became less frequent. The hours turned into days which turned into weeks, until, eventually, I couldn't remember the last time I had a panic attack.

I no longer live in fear of my anxiety. I still have moments where I can feel myself becoming anxious, but it no longer sends me into a panic. I have processes in place and I work through them. I have come to identify the source of my anxiety and determine whether I am in a life-or-death situation or whether I am merely responding to the stressful environment I'm in.

I have trained my brain to recognise that not all moments of stress need to be met with panic. I allow myself to feel what I am feeling, but also acknowledge that this is a moment in time and it will pass.

I have learnt to show myself kindness, understanding and love.

CHANTAL BURLING

Born in South Africa, Chantal immigrated to Australia with her parents and younger brother when she was ten years old. Adjusting to life in Australia came with its own set of challenges, and learning to navigate life in a small country town where she spoke differently from everyone else was tricky.

Growing up with only her immediate family in Australia, Chantal considers her family and friends to be most important to her. She currently lives in sunny Queensland with her husband and two young children.

For most of her life, Chantal has dealt with anxiety, depression and PTSD, and it is because of these struggles that Chantal founded her business, Mindful Mumma Designs.

With her love of art and creating, Chantal created affirmation cards and wall prints with hand-painted and handwritten designs, which she hopes will inspire and encourage people to live their best lives.

Her mission in life is to bring awareness to mental health and to reduce the stigma and criticism surrounding it. Her hope is that one day in the not so distant future, people suffering from mental health issues will no longer feel ostracised and less than because of their mental health.

Chantal is a certified reiki practitioner and has completed a certificate in mindfulness for children. She is currently working towards a certification in emotional freedom technique (EFT) and thought field therapy (TFT).

Website: mindfulmummadesigns.com

YOUR PATH TO HAPPINESS

Danni Vee

HAPPINESS – an emotional state characterised by feelings of joy, satisfaction, contentment and fulfilment.

Do you feel like you are lacking in any of these areas?

Is it a struggle for you to feel joy, satisfaction, contentment or fulfilment every single day?

We live in a world of duality. For one opposite to exist, the other must also exist. When life is fast, there is also the opportunity of it being slow. So can we really have busy without being calm? Not a chance! However we CAN shift busy and step into happiness.

And this is my intention for you to do effortlessly by the end of this chapter.

I have a strong belief that if we change our language and the way we speak about ourselves to ourselves and others, we can create anything we desire in our lives.

So to start this chapter I would love for you to reflect on these powerful questions:

Who are you?

What are your thoughts about yourself?

What are your beliefs?

How do you feel about yourself?

Are you confident in who you are?

Do you feel you deserve to be happy?

YOUR HAPPINESS CAN ONLY GROW TO THE EXTENT YOU DO

I once lived in a world that felt like it was spiralling all around me. I would tell myself and everyone around me, 'I'm busy, I don't even have time for myself.' And you know what, I manifested that into my life tenfold! Things always felt chaotic. It even got to the point of weekly, sometimes daily, meltdowns because I NEVER served myself and chose to stay in that state of mind of BUSY. I could never understand when others wouldn't include me or even reach out for help and then they would share with me, 'Oh, I know how busy you are, I didn't want to bother you.' This made me feel unhappy and isolated. I felt alone in every circle I was a part of.

I chose to stay in the zone of being 'busy' because it was my comfort zone. Choosing to always BE the busy person was where I felt safe, but very rarely truly happy.

When I look back on those times now, I was NEVER really happy, always looking for reasons why I couldn't have downtime (subconsciously, of course) and even judgemental of other women who would put their own needs first, thinking it was easy for them.

This was a state of mind that built up over the years. It first started as a state of survival when I was in an emotionally and mentally abusive relationship with my then-husband. I wanted to protect my children so I would take them everywhere with me, never giving myself the opportunity to just be me. He would make me feel terrible for even going to work without my children, so I would always be juggling two roles in every situation I was in, even in my workplace. I was the martyr, the victim and even the rescuer of my life. I chose to stay and listen to this negative talk for many many years, which soon became my own negative self-talk. I chose to become this woman that was always BUSY so she didn't feel selfish or ever appear to be looking after her own needs. I was worried what others would think of me if I wasn't busy all the time.

I became more and more busy to avoid the guilt, shame and unhappiness growing and thriving within me. Busy to avoid the self-loathing self-talk that was always hiding in the quietness of not being 'busy'.

I filled my days with work, activities for the kids, cleaning the house, cooking meals in advance – anything that would allow me to avoid what was actually going on inside. I served everyone else and never gave an ounce of love and happiness to myself. Stopping was too painful.

BUSY IS OFTEN AN AVOIDANCE OF WHAT IS REALLY GOING ON INSIDE

After many years of self-development and choosing to discover what was really going on, I CHOSE to shift my mindset. I took the time to sit with my demons that actually found pleasure in me staying stuck in this pain and exhaustion of 'busyness' – the demons that made me feel safe in such a hostile inner environment.

As I grew as a person and developed the skills to step into a life that is FULL – not busy – true happiness started bubbling up from the inside. By healing my past hurts and transitioning into a more grounded and powerful state of mind, I was able to step away from the woman married to an abusive husband, into an empowered, healed woman that lived a full life on her own terms. It was an exciting time when I said goodbye to hiding behind busyness and stepped into my true authentic happiness.

I was able to step into being a calm and centred role model for my children. A better coach for my incredible clients, and don't even get me started on how wonderful my love life became with my now-husband. By letting go of the unease of stillness, I was able to embrace the feminine within me and bring true balance into my life.

You, too, can have this with the simple steps at the end of this chapter.

HEALING YOUR PAST ALLOWS YOU TO TRULY STEP INTO YOUR FUTURE AS THE HAPPY POWERFUL WOMAN YOU CHOOSE TO BE!

I have worked with many women throughout the years who strongly believe that they can't have happiness in their life. The judgement and guilt of even starting to prioritise their own wellbeing would bring them to a state of overwhelm and sadness. Choosing happiness just never felt like an option for their life.

Let me introduce you to a beloved client of mine who, before she came to me, was overwhelmed with her life. BUSY building her career, looking after her kids, being a good mother, daughter and friend to EVERYONE, she was constantly giving herself to others, and at the end of the day, she had nothing left to give to herself. She reminded me of how I used to be.

When we first started working together, Julie was depleted of all energy, she lacked internal trust and any self-confidence or belief in herself to find happiness again.

I introduced one of my favourite mindset techniques – thought work – to Julie to start creating a better relationship with herself and then in turn with those around her.

Thought work is a life-changing practice. I believe the thoughts we continuously think about ourselves and the environment around us are a choice and a habit. It is all about remembering that we have a say in the thoughts we habitually think! Thought work involves a series of questions to create awareness and to shine light on what is really going on. Before then, we don't know what we don't know, so you are not aware of the choices you have or don't have.

Thought work begins with starting to question the thoughts that are no longer serving you. When thought work is repeated on a daily basis, you STOP believing everything you think. (I have included the questions I ask my clients to journal on in the action section at the end of this chapter.)

Once Julie truly implemented this practice into her life, she was able to set loving boundaries, starting with herself. Shifting from thoughts like, *I don't have any time for me,* to, *I can make fifteen minutes for myself every single day.* Small steps which created BIG RESULTS.

For Julie, the practice of thought work created a much more harmonious inner world, which rippled out to the world around her. It's not that her world changed, but the way she perceived her world began to shift as she reframed her thoughts about her worth and her ability to set boundaries with herself and those around her.

THOUGHT WORK CAN REFRAME YOUR REALITY AND ALLOW YOU TO EMBODY TRUE HAPPINESS

You see, once you start feeling worthy, you will automatically want to set loving boundaries so that you can give YOU the calm, happiness and empowerment you want in your life.

One thing that thought work IS NOT … is rainbows and unicorns. What I mean by this is that it is important to remember that any kind of mindset work involves ACTION. Julie succeeded in stepping into true happiness because she took the action required to rewire her brain.

If you take intentional action towards your goals every single day, you will create a life of true happiness and wellbeing. Repetition is also a very important part of creating new thought processes. Repetition enables your unconscious mind to bring in the new self-serving habit and unconscious thought patterns that create what you desire in your life. Thought work enables you to make your unconscious conscious.

CREATING HAPPINESS & CALM IN YOUR LIFE REQUIRES ACTION

Caroline was in a similar situation. Caroline was in complete overwhelm due to the busyness of her life. She said she hated her life and the way it was heading, even considering leaving her husband because of the unhappiness engulfing her life.

Caroline and I worked together, and during this time we discovered she was carrying a lot of negative stories and habits from her family that was creating this state of busy, overwhelm and unhappiness.

Sharing her story of how she couldn't make time for herself because she HAD to do everything at home on top of working full-time, she felt unappreciated and undervalued in every area of her life.

We uncovered two of Caroline's highest VALUES which were respect and connection. She discovered that she was not aligned with her true values due to her lack of clear communication with herself and others. Caroline found she was always feeling unhappy and in a space of being 'busy'.

When I challenged Caroline as to why she was choosing busy instead of respect and connection, she shared that she felt uncomfortable having the conversations with her loved ones on how she felt. She felt this way because when she was younger she was often told to 'stop being so emotional' or to 'just be quiet and help the family'. Through these experiences she learnt to hide her feelings and just do what others wanted.

Under my supervision, Caroline worked through these limiting beliefs and stories she was running in her unconscious mind. She CHOSE to step into the uncomfortable until it became comfortable for her. She is now living a fulfilled and happy life where she feels loved, respected and continues to grow on the beautiful connections around her including a now stronger relationship with her husband. Caroline chose to shift from busy to happy.

Everything new is uncomfortable in the beginning. The unknown of what is coming next. The discovery of old limiting beliefs that are keeping you stuck from living your happiest life. It's true you will have to walk through this uncomfort zone, but if you stick with the uncomfortableness, you will eventually move through to the other side and say hello to happiness.

ON THE OTHER SIDE OF YOUR DISCOMFORT ZONE IS YOUR KEY TO HAPPINESS

Do you know what the most beautiful thing about this is? You will have a new expanded comfort zone, which means you are growing and expanding the wonderful person you already are.

THE ONLY TIME YOU ARE ACTUALLY GROWING IS WHEN YOU ARE UNCOMFORTABLE

There are times in our lives when life just gets BUSY. You have deadlines at work, you are building an empire, you are a new parent or an entrepreneur juggling all the things. The reality is that life has a lot in it.

When you are in this season of life it is even more important to step away from busyness into happiness. Happiness that creates a calm and beautiful effortless flow in your life.

Creating a daily habit of bringing calmness into your day is essential in this season of your life. You can effortlessly do this in just five minutes with breath work, a short walk or even a chat with a good friend.

Whenever I am in this season of my life, I choose to shift my language from 'my life is busy' to 'my life is FULL'. So when I am asked about my day, I share that I have a super full day. This completely shifts my thoughts and the way I show up in my days and in my life. Having a full life enables me (and you) to create healthy habits that will enrich and nourish your life, so that taking action is easier and happiness is a given, no matter how full your day is.

Always remember, YOU are worthy of waking up every single day with embodied happiness. I want this for you and your incredible life!

Below are the actions steps I have embraced in my life and share with my clients to step on the path to happiness for good.

ACTION STEPS:

1. Journal my signature awareness questions to start opening your mind to possibilities of embodying happiness:
   - Who are you?
   - What are your thoughts about yourself?
   - What are your beliefs?
   - How do you feel about yourself?
   - Are you confident in who you are?
   - Do you feel you deserve to be happy?
2. Implement the habit of **thought work** into your life to shift your thoughts into a more powerful self-serving creation of your reality. Some great questions to ask yourself are:
   - What are the facts [of your story/the situation]?
   - Where did this thought come from?
   - How does this affect me?
   - Is there a more empowering way to think about this?
3. Shift your language to shift your reality. For example, could your life be FULL instead of busy?
4. Find a grounding practice in your day. This could be:
   - Four deep breaths in through your nose and out through your mouth.
   - Get moving. Something as simple as a five-minute walk.
   - Do something that you find FUN – dance, sing loudly to your favourite song, spend quality/present time with your loved ones.
5. TAKE THE ACTION – one small step every day equals one large shift to a reality of complete happiness.

I would love to leave you with this quote before you start digging deep into your happiness action steps and creating a full life you wake up every day excited to live:

> *'There is no path to happiness. Happiness IS the path.'*
> **Buddha**

DANNI VEE

Danni Vee is a speaker, author and mind-body mentor, empowering ambitious women to move from body conscious to body confident in business and in life.

As a certified fitness and nutrition coach, neurolinguisitic practitioner, women's health specialist and mind-body mentor, Danni has grown a motivated and loyal community of women who want to feel confident and strong in their minds and bodies so that they can show up with unstoppable confidence in their business and life.

Danni coaches ambitious career women who are lacking in body confidence and feel like they've tried almost everything to transform their mindset, nutrition and movement so that they can be their true authentic self and reach their biggest goals with unstoppable confidence.

Danni was the winner of AusMumpreneur 2021 GOLD for Wellness & Wellbeing.

THE TRUTH WILL SET YOU FREE

Denise Schelbergen

Looking back at the first forty years of my life, I like to think that I've done quite well for myself. I've had quite an exciting life. I have been able to follow my heart and do the things I truly wanted to do, both personally and professionally. If this is something you want for yourself, I hope my story will make a difference to you and help you to do the same.

When I was a teenager, I quit high school. I was sixteen, found school boring and couldn't even motivate myself to do my homework. When my teachers told me I had to do my fourth year for the third time, I decided it was time to leave. This announcement initially came as a shock to my parents, but after a while they realised I was serious, and we came to an agreement: I would go to a posh boarding school in Bruges to study tourism. My dad always says they turned me into a lady there, and he's right. I don't know what would have become of me if I hadn't gone to that school. A year later, my parents – together with millions of other people around the world – watched me open the door for and welcome the now King Philippe and Queen Mathilde of Belgium to their wedding reception, live on TV.

In my twenties, I began my career in tourism, specialising in luxury travel. I was paid to visit the most incredible and exotic destinations. One highlight was a four-week trip to French Polynesia and the Cook Islands. I was just twenty-four, hopping my way around the islands, staying at five-star hotels with private butlers at my service twenty-four seven. I was served the best champagne on the deck of my overwater bungalow, which I happily sipped while bubbling away in a jacuzzi, enjoying my view of Bora Bora. I mean, really, how does it get any better than this?

Although I was already living my dream life, there was one more dream I just couldn't leave unfulfilled. So in 2012, just before I turned thirty, I finally did something I had talked about doing for a long time: I quit my job, packed up my belongings and moved to the other side of the world. For the first three and a half years, I lived in Taupo, New Zealand. Then, in 2016, I went over to Australia where I wanted to settle down, and within two years I had permanent residency. Amazing! I had achieved everything I had dreamed of, and I was ready for my new life.

This is when things started to change. I had been single for five years, and none of the men I dated saw a long-term future with me. Although I'd never had a strong desire to have children, the possibility of starting a family was increasingly on my mind. But I had spent all my money on travelling and fun things over the years without saving any. In fact, I was in debt after getting my Australian permanent residency – the process had cost me a fortune and I'd maxed out all my credit cards.

So there I was: thirty-five years old, no boyfriend, no children, no savings, $11,000 worth of debt and living in a shared house with a couple who were expecting their first baby. I was not where I thought I would be. I started to feel defeated, lonely and unhappy. I was used to feeling proud of myself for being so independent and determined in following my heart, but now I felt ashamed of myself. Who would want to be in a relationship with someone with no money? I couldn't even afford to go out on dates. *I need to stop spending and grow up,* I told myself.

No more fun things for Denise – it was time to get serious and get my act together. I went from being an adventurous, free-spirited, life-loving young woman to a hardworking no-time-for-anything-other-than-work person.

I worked from early in the morning until midnight six days a week. Weekends didn't exist anymore; I had no time to relax. My days were planned with military precision. In four years, I completed over forty personal and professional development courses, started my own business, set up a microcredit project in Colombia to help communities get out of poverty and became the managing director of a Dutch foundation. Fortunately, despite spending so much of my time working, I also met the love of my life and became a mom to our beautiful baby boy, Luca. I was getting the results I wanted, but I was extremely busy with no time for anything else.

Then one day, my mentor, Gabriel, reached out to me. I was working with him and his business partner, Scott, on the launch of a transformational leadership program in Australia. Someone in the team had expressed their concerns about me and asked whether Gabe could offer me some support. I'm thankful he did – I wasn't doing well at all. I was exhausted, had no energy left in my body and continuously felt overwhelmed. My mind was forcing me to keep going, but I lacked the strength to fulfil all my commitments. I was suffering and felt resigned.

Gabe said to me, 'Denise, do you know about the US Marines? They are the most effective organisation in the world. When they say something is going to happen, it is going to happen. Do you know why they are so effective? It's because they give every employee, from the bottom to the top, only three accountabilities, and that's all they focus on. It is scientifically proven that people with more than three accountabilities will lose focus and are less effective in producing the results they want. Would you like to have a look at your accountabilities?'

I started to write them all down and came to a total of nine: my son, my relationship with my partner, my business, my role as managing director, my health and wellbeing, my and my partner's family, the sales and marketing course I was in, the transformational leadership program I was launching and breastfeeding Luca.

Gabe then asked, 'If you had to pick three accountabilities, which ones would you choose?'

I took a deep breath and said, 'Number one is Luca. A shared number two' – I cheated a bit – 'is my relationship with my partner and my health and wellbeing. Without those two things working well, none of the projects I'm working on even matter.'

'Okay good, and what is number three?'

'Number three would be my business,' I said.

But I hadn't even finished my sentence when I felt this intense pressure on my solar plexus, as if someone had put their fist on my chest and pushed it so hard that I couldn't breathe. As soon as the words had left my mouth, both Gabe and I said simultaneously, 'No, that's not it.'

I had been speaking with my mind, not with my soul. My body had clearly told me something different, and it was too loud to ignore.

'Number three is not my business,' I said to Gabe. 'I love seeing the results my clients get from working with me, but *I* don't experience joy from it myself. In fact, I really don't like what I am doing, and if I am really honest with you, I only started it because I didn't know what else to do. Someone once told me I'd be really good at this, and I am, but I did it because I didn't know anything else. I took on this person's idea and have built my whole business around that. Everything I do feels forced and is hard work. I don't want to do it anymore.'

Yikes, what a confession! I really didn't see that coming, but as soon as I had said it out loud, a huge burden fell from my shoulders and I felt so relieved.

It was clear – it didn't even matter anymore what number three was. My unexpected admission was a total game changer. I knew now what to do, and I began to systematically work through my list of accountabilities. I looked at every one, asked myself if it truly brought me joy or if I was just trying to please someone else or do what I thought was expected of me, and then decided what I wanted to do. I also asked myself whether I was the only person who could do the job or whether other people could do it for me. If other people could do it for me, I asked for support and delegated my work. The only actions I took were actions focused on my top three priorities and accountabilities.

I shared what had happened with my partner and told him I wanted to spend at least 50% of my time with our son – that I wanted to have the weekends free to spend time together, do fun things, hang out with family and friends, and that I wanted to pivot in my business. Within less than a week, life started to change. At the time, Luca was waking up crying three times a night. We had no idea why, but it wouldn't stop. Two days after my conversation with Gabe, he started sleeping through the night. What a miracle! I could finally sleep, and I started to feel better.

For the launch of my microcredit project in Colombia, I had to raise USD 30,000 and needed to write over forty letters to request money from other foundations. I asked my team for help. We ended up sharing the work, which meant twenty hours of work less for me and feeling more supported than I had ever felt before.

It kept on like this, as if the universe had been waiting to give me all these things but couldn't because I was so busy forcing myself to do things that didn't bring me joy. In only six days I went from being super busy, exhausted and overwhelmed, to being happy, rested and excited about my life.

Since then, I have taken on new practices to help me keep it that way. I would love to share these with you so you can use them in your own life:

1. I now *only* practice listening to my body, and I ignore the chatter in my mind. My solar plexus has become my second brain. It speaks

a truth that comes from a place of deep, inner wisdom – it knows what is best for me. Where in your body is your second brain? Start listening to it. This can take courage, but start practising with simple things, such as asking your body what it wants to eat. If you feel it react negatively to what you suggest, don't eat it.

2. I tell myself the truth, no matter how bad I feel about it or how much I want the truth to be different. Telling myself the truth about my business is what set me free and enabled me to create a joyful and fulfilled life, regardless of what anyone else thought. It even became the inspiration for my new business.

3. I don't take on more than four accountabilities: three big ones and one for fun if it's something that inspires and energises me. I choose them by asking myself the question, *Does it bring me joy?* If the answer is no, I don't do it. Take some time to slow down and really examine what you want to spend your time on, not what you feel you should do or is expected of you. Look out for warning signals to avoid getting stuck in the busyness trap again, such as feelings of overwhelm and resentment, complaining and a busy mind that can't seem to focus.

4. For any request, I give myself twenty-four hours before I need to get back to the person – I let them know that I need to check my calendar first and that I will get back to them tomorrow. That gives me time and space to tune in with my body in the evening, when I have time for myself, and consider what *I* want. I now say 'no' more often than I say 'yes'. If you are a people-pleaser like me and your default answer is 'yes' because you feel guilty about saying 'no', practice with this.

5. I still have many projects, but I stopped doing all the work myself. I created teams around me, and now I only do what only I can do. What can be done by others, I delegate. I do this in a way that's a win-win for everyone involved. For example, my mother-in-law

now looks after my son two days a week, helps us with cooking and cleans our home. She loves cleaning and spending time with us and Luca. We love spending time with her and we can have Luca at home instead of sending him to day care. Because we don't have to clean or cook, we now have more quality time together.

The biggest lesson I learned from all of this is to slow down and allow myself the time to explore and discover what I really want my life to be about. Previously, I had thought my life needed to look a particular way and that I needed to have achieved certain things, but I was wrong. All that matters is that I love my life, nurture the relationships with the people I care about and make sure that my partner and my son have everything they need. Whatever life throws at me in the future, if my relationships with those who matter are healthy and nourished, I can get through anything.

Flow and joy came back into my life with ease as soon as I told myself the truth and stopped forcing things. I now know that when something feels like hard work, I need to stop and look at why that is instead of forcing myself to keep going. Telling myself the truth gave me so much power and freedom. Before, it felt uncomfortable to act on what I said I was going to do. But now, I have created a life where each day is filled with lots of little moments that make me feel intensely happy and grateful for everything I have.

DENISE SCHELBERGEN

Denise Schelbergen has over twenty years of experience in product and business development in experiential luxury travel. She is a social entrepreneur and futurist committed to ending poverty and empowering people around the world to live their lives to the fullest. She is the managing director and board member of the Dutch foundation Kula Loans, the founder and CEO of the Australian-based coaching and consulting business The Ikigai Entrepreneur and a co-author of the book *Goodbye Busy, Hello Happy*.

In 2019, Denise began a passion project in Colombia. In collaboration with her local partner, she helps families who live on less than a few dollars a day, with no clean drinking water, sanitation or electricity, to get out of poverty for good and create a new future. Through a four-phase poverty alleviation model, participants create a business plan (with the aid of local business experts) and receive investment and mentoring to help them succeed. In the same year, Denise founded her business The Ikigai Entrepreneur, providing transformational programs and workshops for socially conscious leaders who want to live a purposeful life that makes a difference in the world. She also offers retreats for emerging and advanced leaders who want to lead with impact, that bring together her experiences in coaching and consulting, luxury travel and social work in Asia, Latin America and Africa.

Denise has always gone after what she wants in life and believes that anyone can do the same – if they have the courage to overcome their inauthentic fears. Not every transformation journey will be easy or glamorous. Not every story will be the stuff of movies or fairytales. But when you get to the other side, a more fulfilling and authentic future will be waiting for you. Denise believes that a life of freedom, joy and fulfilment is within everyone's reach, but we often need a helping hand to grasp hold of it.

Website: theikigaientrepreneur.com
Email: denise@theikigaientrepreneur.com

LET'S GET CURIOUS ...
AND THEN GET BRAVE
Fiona Luca

How does one define busy?

How does one quantify what happiness is?

Interpretation and perception really are everything, and it is our personal experience of life and the programs we have adopted as little people that, in fact, determine the answers to the above questions.

I don't feel called to spend the entire next chapter talking neuroscience, but what I do feel intuitively and ever so passionately called to do is evoke curiosity, self-reflection and a fire in your belly, one that inspires you to take action and move closer to a life that not only affords you time, space and alignment, but one that verifies what HAPPY looks and FEELS like for you.

> *'Happiness is when what you think, what you say*
> *and what you do are in harmony.'*
> **Mahatma Gandhi**

Let's go back a step ... I am Fiona Luca, an innate seeker, mother of two precious children and a lifelong student committed to expanding and growing to the most embodied and effervescent version of myself in this lifetime.

My professional hats are varied and colourful (a little like my wardrobe!).

My entrepreneurial spirit is committed to my work in mind-body therapy, yoga, dance, Pilates and anything movement based. As a business coach and consultant, podcast host and youth mentor, I position mindfulness, movement and mindset at the centre of my offerings.

Why?

Because we are not single dimensional, there are multiple dimensions to our existence – mind, body, heart and sooul – and my mission is to inspire you to encourage them all to converse and essentially 'like' each other ... a lot!

In 2017 I made a big decision, one that has changed the course of my life in more ways than I could ever have imagined.

I sold a business.

Not just any business, but rather, one that was birthed, cradled, nurtured and fuelled with every inch of my being for almost twelve years.

I planted the seed of this business long before it was a living and breathing entity.

My dream was to always be a teacher. Not necessarily in a conventional way, but one that left an imprint on every student's life I touched.

Aligned with this dream was a deep-seeded passion for dance, one that had been fostered since the age of three.

Marrying my love for dance and a deep desire to teach created a clear pathway to what came next: a performing arts studio – that would change the world, of course!

This business model had meaning for me. Every action was inspired and fuelled by passion and complete commitment, and I wholeheartedly believe that because of this, when I opened the doors in partnership in

2006, the rest took care of itself … for a period of time!

At that stage, I didn't have the awareness nor introspection to acknowledge how much of my 'programming' and limiting beliefs were driving this endeavour. As the years progressed and the partnership ended, I started to feel the doors closing in, even while the business grew exponentially.

I started to feel lost. Lost in the pressures and 'busyness' of running my business. Lost in my world outside of the business, and most certainly disconnected from my own self – my inner world.

Hours rolled into days, months and years, and I started having incessant moments of realisation (they started as whispers, of course). Realisation that the undertone of my existence was overwhelm, despair, stress, anxiety and a sense of loss.

Ironically, I had gained so much since my business journey began; a loyal and supportive community, financial stability, security and reputation. Yet what was lost was my sense of self, my identity, as it was completely wrapped up in the brand I was so committed to building.

What hurt the most was the realisation that I had, in fact, followed in the same footsteps as my mother. The ones she herself wishes she had the awareness and strength to change direction of.

As the mother of a two-year-old and with one on the way, combined with what was once a quiet voice inside that had now turned into a constant scream for help, I was left with what I felt was the 'only' option; the only option, not just as a business owner, but as a mother.

I sold the business.

IS THIS THE PART WHERE MY LIFE TURNED FROM BUSY TO HAPPY?

Well, admittedly this was the first step to move me in that trajectory … I was certainly a much more aligned, integrous and less stressed version of myself.

But the short answer … NO …

The next part is where YOU have to get involved. The reader, the enquirer, the curious person on the other side of this page.

What quickly followed my exit as business owner was a deep dive into this murky brown, liminal space. The one we all fear so much.

There was uncertainty, potential regret and grief, but the emotion that was most pressing was emptiness, or for a better word, lack of identity.

How on earth, as a thirty-six-year-old mother, wife and accomplished business owner, did I NOT know who I was?

I was confident, capable and successful, yet why on Earth was I beginning to question every belief, value, relationship and outcome I had identified as 'my own', as me, Fiona?

Because no-one in my 'circle' at that time was committed to building self-awareness or encouraging me to get curious and ask those BIG questions, nor reinforcing that those incessant 'whispers' matter.

And I most certainly did not have the tools or resources to work it out on my own!

As a society, we are well conditioned to attach – to outcomes, to concepts, to people and to trends.

We are also well conditioned to 'suck it up' and get on with it!

'The pull of the future is as real as the pressure of the past.'
Arthur Kostler

What is not reiterated is how programmed we are (for nearly 95% of our day) to create a lifestyle that is aligned with our inherited belief systems and the patterns we learnt and adopted as young people, based on our experience and learnings from our primary caregivers and environments.

Nor are we ever really encouraged to 'FEEL' our way through life.

Think first, act later, they say!

Where do our thoughts come from?

Our programming, most of which is not even OURS!

What can our bodies tell us?

Well, everything, if we listen – it NEVER lies.

So to connect the dots, is it any wonder, now that I had dissociated from my 'identity' as Fiona Luca, director of a successful business, I felt so bloody disconnected and lost?

What I had afforded myself was time and stillness … and when we do that, we create space.

Space to see, listen, and if we are brave enough, to hear …

It wasn't being 'BUSY' that made me unhappy, it was living unconsciously, misaligned from my values and deep desires, that was making me unhappy.

So let's get curious together and then get clear …

If it feels comfortable and safe, I'd love to invite you to deep dive into these responses.

- When was the last time you did a revision of your values?

And let's take it one step further and ask, did you question if those values were even yours, and if so, how often do you LEAD by them (rather than merely identify with them)?

- What is meaningful to you?
- What do you know of yourself to be true?
- And is the picture you display to the outside world congruent with the version of yourself inside?

As a business and life coach and mentor, I urge my clients to start to SEE themselves objectively, rather than attach to the baggage we have packed and gathered.

I can already see you starting to panic over the copious amounts of 'baggage' you have suddenly identified with, but please don't fear, we all have truckloads of this 'baggage business'. What's important is recognising it and doing something about it.

That's the 'seeing' component right there, which I refer to as self-awareness.

For such a good portion of our lives we are reacting rather than responding to our world.

Throughout our lives (and previous lives, if you're into that), we have acquired so much conditioning, so many beliefs, so many ideas that are not even ours.

Our parents, teachers, mentors, friends, society and life experiences have all imprinted memorable information in our minds that we use on a daily basis to dictate how we show up in the world.

The more self-aware we become (this has nothing to do with age, by the way!), the more we develop the capacity to question these inherited belief systems and question whether they belong to us, serve us or honour our truth.

From here we reclaim choice. Choice to make decisions and take action in a way that *does* align with our truth.

This is potentially the most profound revelation I have acquired post the sale of my business.

How often are you 'reacting' to your world and how often are you 'responding'?

Reactivity is the more than likely 'old' stuff.

For me, whilst running my business, I was intensely lacking boundaries.

Responding to emails and messages at inappropriate hours of the day, over-committing to my clients, staff and students, subconsciously micromanaging my team in an effort to take some of the 'burden' off of them.

Hindsight tells me that these were all telltale signs of my lack of value and worth of myself, particularly of myself in my role as director.

I needed to PROVE day in and day out that I was worthy of that title, rather than believing in myself that I was, and executing it well!

My porous boundaries were a subconscious effort to be 'SEEN' and validated.

They had nothing to do with my business or what was happening in my business. They were a direct reflection of my own scarcity and lack mentality.

Every complaint (and they were few and far between), I treated as a direct reflection of my own 'lack of ability or success'.

Every time a student left, I wanted to BE more and DO more as this was a direct reflection of how my business wasn't enough, or how it (I) had failed.

With every feat came the anxiety and pressure of could I ever do it that good again?

Can you see here how my reactivity was constantly affirming my own sense of lack?

And I can assure you that when we approach anything in our lives, albeit professionally or personally, from a place of lack and scarcity, we never find the joy in the experience as we are completely reliant on the outcome to provide us with this.

Responding would have involved me objectively looking at each scenario and building perspective around what it was actually teaching me, void of how I 'felt' about it or how it 'made me feel'.

Responding would have also afforded me a chance to 'understand' the scenario from another perspective – that of my clients, students and staff.

Can you see how much more powerful THAT process would have been?

How much more space I would have had to respond effectively and supportingly for everyone involved and how that experience wouldn't have taken from my cup but rather afforded me a lesson of growth?

So I ask you again, how often are you reacting to your world and how often are you responding?

And is this reactivity relevant to the actual experience, or are you latching onto something else to define this experience?

So let's use the word 'busy' as a reactive response.

Think about how often we respond using this word, and how easy it is to default to 'busy' mode.

What is 'busy' trying to tell us?

How does 'busy' fuel our ego, or camouflage challenge or discomfort?

Why do we insist on 'filling' our days at work, at home and our dialogue with this concept?

What is 'busy' distracting us from?

I have spoken about the power of creating space and reclaiming choice to build self-awareness, so let's all have a collective light-bulb moment here and recognise how 'busy' does not allow for either of these.

It narrows our vision. Closes us in.

My body feels suffocated simply writing this.

How on earth is one able to access the freeing feeling of joy and happiness in this state?

This isn't about turning your back on your mission, or downsizing your impactful empire or leaving your husband and children and flying to the Maldives indefinitely, this is about building awareness around the WHY behind our busyness.

The WHY behind your pace …

We cannot possibly say goodbye to the concept of busy without building curiosity around it and making peace with what it is representing.

So with your permission, I am going to take a trip around the roundabout and connect the dots of my experience above with a little clarity and a whole lot of transparency.

As I have humbly expressed, I spent a really large portion of my time as a business owner in a scarcity mindset, not a leaders mindset, and this was due to my own belief system – that I had to be more in order for people to believe in me, but more importantly, to love me.

My reactivity, my incessant pressure on myself and my burning desire to constantly BE more was because I didn't believe, deep down, that I was enough, not for my business, my community or for myself.

As I was drowning in my busyness I was distracting myself from seeing my truth, because I was scared – fear stricken, in fact.

Two and a half years after I sold my business, my marriage broke down.

With the time and space my business sale afforded me, I had the capacity to truly see what was going on – my truth.

In a desperate attempt to seek wholeness, worthiness, acceptance, validation, success and ultimately happiness through my business, I was deflecting my ability to acknowledge and accept the lack I was experiencing in my relationship.

'Lack' of happiness, of joy, was resonant in two key relationships in my life: my relationship to my business and my relationship to my husband.

Each of which fuelled the other.

Are these two huge life choices interconnected?

I believe YES, with every inch of my heart.

Was it necessary for me to experience both to access the genuine inner peace I now believe I have?

I believe YES, with every inch of my heart.

Have I said goodbye to busy and hello to happy in my own world?

What I have done is grieved, made peace with and accepted my journey. I have stepped forward with the spaciousness and curiosity to make daily choices to nurture the Fiona I choose to be.

For she CHOOSES to be content.

If this chapter can ignite anything in you, let it be curiosity and bravery.

The curiosity to explore all of the beautiful pillars of yourself and see with clarity the roses but also the stems.

And the bravery to start asking those tough questions that ignite us to access the truth of who we are.

It is from here that you will steer away from BUSY and define what happiness is for YOU.

FIONA LUCA

Growing up in a family dedicated to small business and having built and sold successful businesses herself, Fiona Luca is no stranger to the hard work that comes with entrepreneurship and the creative depths that have to be reached to create the kind of environment that truly helps clients level up and move to take action.

A renowned performer, dancer, choreographer, business owner, mind-body therapist and coach sharing her own story, Fiona is a creative practitioner driven to support women and youth of all ages facing the same challenges she has faced in the past.

In 2017, Fiona stepped down as director of a thriving business. After winning the Victorian Musical Guild and People's Choice Awards and being nominated for an Australian Business Women of the Year in the Geelong region, she took some time off to focus on her young family and get back to what it was that really moves her soul. Fiona founded Move with Fiona Luca to serve those wanting to reclaim their power and choice when life has become all consuming.

To help women and business owners reconnect with their soul's purpose after leading a conventional life, Fiona positions mindfulness, movement and mindset at the centre of her offering. Move with Fiona Luca operates bespoke group and one-on-one programs, inviting participants to star in their wellness journey and take their personal and professional development to new heights.

In keeping with her love of mentoring and inspiring the health and wellbeing of young generations, Fiona launched the *Talking Youth* podcast in 2020, to give young people a platform where they can speak out and be heard.

LEARNING TO CHERISH RATHER THAN CONTROL

Fleur Chambers

It was a regular Tuesday afternoon in the autumn of 2011. The sun's rays were gentle, casting shadows across my lawn. I was standing barefoot in my back garden, cool grass nestled between my toes, talking to my mum on the phone. My children (one, two and four years old at the time), were enjoying filling buckets with soil and water. It was both joyful and messy.

The conversation between my mother and I followed its usual trajectory. I'd share my 'news'. Tom, my eldest son, had brought a painting home from his new kindergarten. Gabe was learning to ride his blue scooter. Dash, my youngest, had decided that bum-shuffling was a better way to keep up with his older brothers than learning to crawl.

My family had just moved across town to a new neighbourhood. It was a beautiful part of the world, but for now, I was yet to establish any real connections.

My mum and I had phoned each other at least once a week for most of my adult life. However, over recent months, there was a new addition to our familiar chats – my tears. Sometimes, the tears would come from sleep-deprivation, other times from the pressure I placed on myself to be a perfect mother. There were times when the tears flowed after receiving my mother's kindness, love and understanding. On this day, the strong flow of emotion stemmed from a conversation I'd just had with a stranger in the park.

This man – another parent – had shared, with great honesty and vulnerability, the fears he held for his child who had a disability. I can't remember how we moved from small talk to such a deep conversation, but at one point, he looked me in the eyes and asked, 'Who will look after my son when I die?' I had no idea how to reply to him. At that moment, I wished I could take his pain away.

As I repeated this story to my mother, warm tears were streaming down my face. I knew, at an intellectual level, it wasn't my responsibility to provide this distressed stranger with an answer to his question, but his words sat like a twenty-pound weight on my heart. It felt hard to breathe.

At the time, it felt like everyone, both friends and strangers, had a painful story to share with me. Everywhere I looked there was a heaviness – and collective sadness. It felt like the autumn breeze carried with it the energy of fear. Each of these interactions would stay with me, like a shadow I couldn't shake. I'd be bathing the kids, reading their bedtime stories or tidying the house, and these stories would be playing like a record on repeat in my mind.

As I write this, Australia (and the entire world) is coming out of a turbulent period of lockdowns, restrictions and pandemic living. Fear and uncertainty have been the pervasive culture over the last few years. I know many of you will relate to this feeling of being surrounded by stories that pull at your heartstrings and make you feel an uncomfortable combination of compassion and helplessness.

Ever since I was a child, I've been extremely compassionate. When I was eight years old, I would say a little prayer each time I heard the siren of an ambulance, sending my best wishes to whoever was on their way to hospital.

I spent much of my twenties working at a large not-for-profit organisation, providing support for people experiencing disadvantage, including disability. During this time, I was surrounded by examples of how life could be hard, unfair and painful for people. But I also felt hopeful and able to see the joy in the world too.

I have always been ready and willing to offer a shoulder to cry on, being someone people naturally confide in. What had changed in recent times was my response to the stories that people were sharing with me. It was beginning to feel uncalibrated and too strong to handle. I felt like a tree without roots, being blown about by the wind and the rain that was other people's lives, engulfed in a cloud of generalised fear and heaviness.

My mum, who knows me better than anyone, had noticed the heightened sensitivity growing within me. During this phone call, she seized her moment and said to me in a firm but loving voice, 'Darl, you really need to start practicing mindfulness, so you can feel stronger and more resilient for yourself, others and those three gorgeous kids of yours.'

Growing up, Mum was a psychologist who, to her credit, refrained from 'putting me on the therapist's couch' too often. Over the years, she had suggested I try mindfulness, but this time her words landed in a different way. I felt desperate. Maybe this would be the answer. So began my journey into mindfulness and meditation, my transition from busy to happy.

Eleven years later, I look back at that version of myself – the busy, tired and hypersensitive mother – and I notice three interrelated things:

1. My self-imposed high expectations. My desire to be a perfect mother, my desperate attempts to keep my kids happy and to control life had created stress in my body, distraction within my mind and a heaviness within my heart.

2. My negative perspective. Over time, living this way was like putting on

a pair of sunglasses with lenses that were tinted with fear. The longer I wore these glasses, the more sad stories I would see and hear, until my perspective of the world became skewed towards the negative. As each day passed, a growing belief that the world was not a safe place sank deep into my bones. And so, the cycle of control and fear continued.

3. I was desperately lonely. Yes, lonely! A strange thing to consider given I was never alone. In fact, during that period in my life, there was always a little person on my hip or at my side, even when I went to the bathroom. I now know that this loneliness was a call home to my deeper nature. It was an invitation back into my body, my heart and an abiding sense that the world, despite its challenges, was a safe place. It was a gentle whisper to loosen my grip and instead, to begin to trust life.

I wonder if there are elements of this story that you can relate to? Maybe you know deep in your heart that the high expectations you place on yourself (as a mother, sister, daughter, friend, colleague, business owner) are making you stressed, anxious or overwhelmed? Or is it the expectations you are placing on others or how your life *should* look that are causing this contraction within you?

Perhaps you can identify with the feeling of being deeply affected by the state of the world? Does watching the news or hearing about the challenges of family or friends impact your wellbeing and sense of resilience?

Are you ready to be less self-critical and more kind and compassionate towards yourself? Or do you just want to get off the hamster wheel of never-ending to-do lists so you can actually enjoy the life that is here right now?

Over the last eleven years, I've explored many different ways to bring mindfulness, compassion and warm-hearted curiosity into my life, so that I can experience the type of happiness that feels real and sustainable. A version of happiness that looks more like saying 'yes' to your entire life – the joys and the challenges, and less like chasing a perfect life (an imaginary place free of disappointment, regret or any other uncomfortable emotion).

Along the way, some practices have become like old and loyal friends, ready to support me whatever my circumstance. They've helped me reorientate my awareness away from business, distraction and fear, towards greater presence, peace and happiness. May they support you along your journey too.

PRACTICE 1 – MORNING GLORY

It's easy to wake up and get straight into *doing mode*, checking your social media or emails, planning, organising yourself and others in your household. Taking a moment to begin your day with presence and possibility will help you feel happier throughout your day. Upon waking, try this short practice before you switch into doing mode.

Begin by taking three deep breaths. As you breathe in, really notice how your chest expands at the front, back and sides. Feel into this sense of physical expansion as you breathe.

Repeat silently in your mind: *Today is a new day filled with possibilities.*

As you continue to breathe in, imagine that you can *invite in* something you would like to experience today (for example: calm, patience, gratitude, love, joy or peace).

As the morning air travels deep into your chest and belly, imagine that it carries with it this quality you would like to experience more of today.

Place your hand on your heart and whisper: *Thank you.*

Where attention goes, energy flows. Trust that you will experience this quality you have just welcomed in today.

PRACTICE 2 – A SAFETY RESET

When you notice yourself becoming distracted, overwhelmed or anxious, pause and try this practice that will calm your nervous system and bring you back into the safety of the present moment – the place where happiness resides.

Find a quiet place to sit at home, maybe on your bed or in the living room.

Begin by simply casting your eye around the space you are in, really noticing the basic features of your environment that provide you with a sense of safety. Perhaps you notice the door, its handle, the windows, the way they open and close, or the roof over your head.

Move your awareness to some of the aspects of your room that allow you to feel comfortable and at home. Maybe there's a photo or picture, an indoor plant, a book or your favourite blanket or jumper. Perhaps the way the sunlight streams in makes you feel relaxed and at ease.

Remind yourself that this space doesn't need to be perfect or even tidy in order to offer you a feeling of safety.

Take a few deep breaths into this moment, really imagining this experience of being safe landing within your body, mind and heart.

Notice any changes in your physical body. Notice any changes in your emotional world.

Repeat silently in your mind: *Right here, right now, I am safe, I am free from harm.*

Offer this moment a smile! You've just recalibrated your nervous system away from busyness and towards happiness. Trust that this safety reset will create positive ripples in your day.

PRACTICE 3 – GRATEFUL BODY SCAN

It's so easy to spend our days being critical of our physical body, ruminating over the way it looks, the parts that wobble, ache or don't work like they used to. When you notice your inner critic get loud, pause and try this powerful gratitude practice.

Find yourself a quiet place to sit. Take a few deep breaths.

Read the lines below out loud or in your mind.

Take a deep breath between each line and really let the words land in your body, mind and heart.

Thank you, mind, for helping me make sense of the world, for allowing me to learn new things, broaden my perspective and solve problems creatively.

Thank you, eyes, for allowing me to see the faces of those I love, the colour of the sky at sunset and the familiar features of my neighbourhood.

Thank you, ears, for offering me the gift of music, laughter and the words spoken by family, friends and the people I admire.

Thank you, mouth, for allowing me to taste and enjoy all different types of food.

Thank you, chest, for knowing exactly how to receive each breath, for taking in fresh oxygen and ridding my body of carbon dioxide.

Thank you, heart, for beating, feeling, loving and reminding me what is true in this world.

Thank you, legs, for taking me where I want to go, for allowing me to move forward in the direction of what truly matters and away from things that aren't important.

Thank you, hands, for helping me carry, hold, embrace and express myself.

Thank you, body, for working all day, every day like a complex but beautiful orchestra, so that I can experience the miracle that is each day on planet Earth.

Well done! This moment of gratitude will make it easier to feel grateful for other aspects of your life too.

PRACTICE 4 – A NATURE FIX

When you notice that your to-do list is getting long and overwhelm or busyness is creeping in, pause, and try this practice. You'll be surprised how it instantly relaxes you and alters your mindset.

Go outside. (Yes, I know you are busy, but you can afford to take two minutes, I promise.)

Take a few deep breaths and engage all your senses. Notice the colours around you, the different sounds, the movement in your environment.

Look up at the sky. Feel the breeze on your skin.

Notice how things are always changing. Noises come and go. Clouds move across the sky.

Remind yourself that life is always changing. The challenges or pressure you are facing today won't always be here.

Notice how nature never hurries, she gets things done with ease and in perfect timing.

Enjoy a few more deep breaths. Be open to the possibility that you can be more like nature, doing what you need to, but in a more relaxed, easygoing way.

Well done! This nature fix will help you move through your day with greater ease.

PRACTICE 5 – EVENING SURRENDER

On an average day, uncomfortable conversations, differences in opinion, endless work emails and heavy traffic all build up and form physical, mental and emotional stress. Learning to *let go* at night is a powerful practice for returning our bodies, minds and hearts to a state of balance and equilibrium before our head hits the pillow. Try this practice to release stress at the end of the day so you can sleep more deeply and wake feeling refreshed.

As you lie in bed, focus on your breath. Notice how your chest rises and falls as you breathe.

Try as best you can to lengthen your exhale. Really allow it to feel long and smooth.

For the next few breaths, count to four on the exhale.

Then ask yourself: *What can I let go right now?* (For example: physical tension, self-criticism, a past conversation, regret or worry).

Imagine this thing leaving your body with each exhale.

Repeat in your mind: *I let go of what no longer serves me so that I may sleep deeply and wake feeling refreshed.*

Swimming against the tide of busyness requires us to pause throughout our day and feel present and safe in our minds, bodies and hearts.

FLEUR CHAMBERS

Fleur Chambers is a multi-award-winning meditation teacher, bestselling author of *Ten Pathways*, creator of *The Happy Habit* app and philanthropist. With over two million downloads in forty countries, Fleur's work is encouraging people from all walks of life to find happiness today, not 'someday when ...'

Using her experience of living with chronic pain, Fleur is helping others to see that happiness isn't an imaginary place free of disappointment, regret, insecurity or any other uncomfortable emotion. In contrast, real happiness is the ability to live wholeheartedly alongside our challenges and to learn from them.

With proceeds from *The Happy Habit* funding grassroots projects in some of the poorest communities around the world, Fleur is using meditation as a tool for social change. She believes that we meditate not only to alleviate our own suffering, but also to improve the lives of people all around the world.

Keen to strengthen your capacity to face your challenges and experience happiness whilst also contributing to the world? Download

The Happy Habit app from the App Store or Google Play, or purchase a copy of *Ten Pathways*.

GROW AGAINST THE GRAIN

Gloria Tabi

'I'm no longer accepting the things I cannot change ...
I'm changing the things I cannot accept.'
Angela Davis

For years, I worked myself to the bone because I didn't feel a sense of belonging at work. I reasoned that the way for me to feel accepted and included was to work twice as hard as everyone else. This self-imposed torment went on for years without easing. It wasn't until I literally couldn't move out of exhaustion that I stopped.

For a long time, I restricted myself to what the world said I am.

A 'Black woman'.

Society has made it that as a 'Black woman', I'm forced to fit into what the world says I am.

I am labelled the 'angry Black woman', yet I am unheard.

I am supposed to stand out by my hair, skin and bone, yet I am unseen.

My race, skin colour, hair and bone structure defined me into a permanent sculpture – just like my birth sex has dictated my gender. I couldn't deviate, and I was feeling boxed in.

A Black woman.

They say, 'You're not very bright.'

They say, 'You're ugly.'

They say, 'You're not meant to lead, so don't try to be ambitious.'

They say, 'The world doesn't care about you, your skills, talents or wellbeing, so don't even try.'

This tape has played over and over in my mind for as long as I've been old enough to read and write. There seemed to be no way around it, and settling with that reality was as painful as trying to contemplate reinventing myself altogether.

What was interesting with this belief playing in my mind was that people around me – my own family, friends and people I looked up to – also believed in this woeful narrative, and they, too, confirmed it to me.

There were times I wanted to run away from them all to block it out and completely find a new version of me, if there could be such a thing.

This was not easy.

Where do you go?

No-one is an island.

We live in communities and in families. But what if all the people around you are also bringing you down?

I ask, *Where do you go?*

I remember experiencing this excruciating burden of weight I'd been carrying for so long and needing desperately to take it off me, but I didn't know how.

Before I could fully articulate the small changes that were starting to happen within me, I knew intensely that I wanted to learn. To learn anything that could help me understand the world I find myself in. I started reading anything and everything I could find from *The 7 Habits of Highly Successful People* by Stephen Covey to Oprah's *What I Know For Sure* and research articles by Du Bois, Frantz Fanon, Angela Davis, Patricia Hill Collins, Shakespeare and many more.

The societal illusional divide, that places some above the line and others below the line, began to make sense. And although I didn't like it, I was beginning to understand the broader societal issues to do with race, gender and racism. I was very dissatisfied to simply accept it!

As I put down building blocks into a range of personal development and self-discovery through learning, my growth accelerated. I attended courses, travelled to retreats and undertook formal training, including research at university.

This intentional devotion of time and energy in self-development exploration started to pay dividends. They weren't only a satisfying feeling to me, but as I continued to embrace the learning each day, I grew.

I didn't just read and absorb, I joined local groups, I served as an executive member for the Parent and Citizen Association of NSW at my local schools and later became a president. Although I still lacked self-confidence, I became determined to face my fears, so I joined a local Toastmasters to put myself to the test and learn to deliver ad hoc and impromptu speeches in front of people I didn't know. I was keen to learn the art of public speaking to build my self-confidence.

This conscious learning, experimentation and experience provided me with opportunities to engage with people completely outside my circle, and this further broadened my network.

> *'The beautiful thing about learning is that no-one*
> *can take it away from you.'*
> **Author unknown**

The self-discovery and power of education was helping me to really know, learn and unlearn, and was now transforming my life. Getting to drive my own destiny was becoming a reality.

Then, something outside my control happened to me. Someone at a place I work decided to remind me that I was still that 'Black woman' and that I was not welcome or entitled to be in the same workspace as them. Their behaviour was vindictive, demeaning and traumatising.

But as I'd been on a journey of self-discovery prior to this awful situation rearing its head, I was becoming much more mature in my outlook and to life itself. Because of this, I went on to make a decision that changed the trajectory of my life as far as my career was concerned.

I knew, in my heart of hearts, that bleak 'Black woman' narrative didn't wash anymore, because I knew so much more about myself and how society is constructed when it comes to my race and people who look like me.

With all my strength, my learnings under my belt and in humility, I stood up straight to the bully and said (even while my voice still shook) they were wrong about me, and that they were not going to get away with their action. I had kept a meticulous diary on the incident and when the time came, I was able to give clear evidence of what had happened. I was able to defend myself. I stood my ground and eventually walked away with no regrets. Such is the power of self-determination!

The incident was dire; it meant I had to walk away from a job and a career I loved. It was indeed a difficult thing to do, and I have recently only begun to understand the enormity of the problem now that I have left and time has passed.

Having someone disrespect you because of who you are is insidious and a painful thing to have to experience because it is, in a sense, denying you of your birthright, your humanity. It has the potential to mess with your very self-esteem and self-worth.

With time, I have gently turned the *pain* into *purpose* and developed courage, confidence and compassion in ways that previously wouldn't have been possible.

Courage to stand up to the malicious person.

Confidence in my own abilities. For the first time, I knew I didn't need a saviour because I had my own strength and resources within me. I was able to mobilise this and use it to defend myself in a way that made sense to me, whilst still acting within my values.

Compassion. Whilst I was going through the ordeal, I started a platform to support others who were also experiencing workplace bullying and racism, to voice their traumas in a safe, kind and caring environment.

During the ordeal, I went on to write and publish my first book, *Inclusive Teams and Workplaces: Everyone Wins!!* I also established a thriving business, EVERYDAY INCLUSION, to help senior executives create outstanding work culture to retain good employees, increase productivity and create a sense of belonging. Turning years of never-ending pain of being a 'Black woman' – unseen and not included at work – into my business purpose.

Then I thought to myself, *Why give your keys away?*

When you have been conditioned to be, think and behave in a certain way, it can be difficult to change suddenly and be something different. The daily work in stripping away layer by layer, narrative by narrative and dialogue by dialogue continued. I noticed, as I mastered one hurdle, there is always another more urgent need which arises … relentlessly.

Somehow, because I continue to battle through the 'Black woman' narrative, my sense of happiness has been dictated by others and the world for so long. Then I came across the quote below, and it changed everything.

'Most people are about as happy as they make up their minds to be.'
Abraham Lincoln

I began to learn that happiness is, in fact, a choice that I can make for myself, no matter what I have or how I feel. I reasoned that if happiness is a choice, then I can make it happen for me, just like I have taken choices regarding learning and self-development for some time. So, instead of ascribing to the 'Black woman' noise, I chose happiness from that day forward.

Like the learning development practice, I began to intentionally seek happiness daily in ways I knew how. I decided I was not going to be held hostage by my circumstances, nor would I seek happiness in the world from possessions – what I have or do not have. I have come to know the world didn't have a 'Black woman's' best interest anyway, so why do I continue to be miserable by it? My happiness was therefore going to be rooted in *me* first, the things I hold dear and lived through by my values.

Once I stopped chasing the world's definition of happiness, I began to see that my decision to experience happiness has been right in front of me all along.

But simply knowing that happiness is a choice was not enough. I had to practise experiencing happiness through everyday conscious decisions in how I lived, moved and experienced life each day. This included the food I chose to nourish my body with to stay strong, well and healthy; the people I chose to invite into my inner circle to live life with; the books I read; the paths I walked; the entertainment I enjoyed – these all became conscious selections. And when I did that, I started to experience more joy.

If you've read this far, I thank you. I will now share habits I have embraced and practised (without fail) over the years for inspiration and guidance as I continue to find joy and happiness *no matter what*. Here are my seven happiness practices in no particular order:

1. WAKE UP HAPPY

I have practised being an early riser, up before the sun, starting my day with yoga. I go to the gym a few times each week, before or after work, to keep my mind and body healthy. I also enjoy the challenges of participating in running and trekking events with my family across the Blue Mountains where we live. I participate in a park run most Saturdays.

This practice helps me to be highly organised, which has been essential in my success as a mother, maintaining a career, starting my own business and hands-on renovating my home, whilst participating in further studies and training – the ultimate juggling act. Every single task on my list has been consciously placed there and brings me some form of joy.

2. COUNT YOUR BLESSINGS

The narratives I've had throughout my life as a 'Black woman' have meant there were times I wished I wasn't on the disadvantaged list. However, that has not been the case, so I choose to focus on the positive aspects of life like being healthy enough that my body allows me to run, which I love, rather than obsessing on the negatives. I set my mind on specific things to be grateful for – my relationship, my children and my family. I work hard to find ways to discover that there is always, *always*, something to be grateful for.

3. CARRY YOUR SMILE IN CONFIDENCE

Ironically 'Black people's' smiles are used as a weapon to dehumanise us. I have been called 'miss smiley, show us your teeth so we can see you' in a derogatory manner.

So, as part of my self-determination journey, I decided that carrying a smile is a wonderful and beautiful thing. Studies also show smiling can have a profound influence over how we feel in our brain. Combining these factors, I choose to carry a smile on my face. This action alone continues to help me to experience and increase my happiness – simply by choosing to smile. Not forgetting all the nice smiles you'll get in return for flashing yours!

4. TREAT OTHERS WELL

The Golden Rule, 'to treat others as you yourself like to be treated', is powerful and carries truth. Deep down we all want to be accepted, included and treated with respect. So, I take this rule seriously and incorporate it into my daily practice. Although, as a 'Black woman', the world seems to think that treating people with dignity and respect doesn't apply to us.

But I choose to exhibit kindness, patience and grace whenever possible without expecting miracles in return. Still, it makes me feel good about myself as a giver of kindness and bringer of joy.

5. FROM PAIN TO PURPOSE

I can't lie, life can be difficult on so many levels. I don't think anyone can completely escape some of life's pain; we will all encounter it at some point. But when you do, try to remind yourself that the tribulations are difficult, but they will pass.

This reminder helps me to search deeper to find the tiniest meaning in the pain.

What can I learn? What is this pain trying to teach me? Through perseverance we can use what we learn in our own trials to support and comfort others in theirs.

6. DAILY AFFIRMATIONS ARE GOD SENT

I love affirmations, especially Louise Hay's ones, which I keep on my desk. They're positive thoughts accompanied with affirmative beliefs and personal statements of truth. I will often recite them throughout the day. They release stress while building your confidence and your general outlook on life.

7. USE YOUR STRENGTHS

Over the years I've been able to identify my natural talents, strengths and abilities. To hone these skills, I've looked for opportunities to utilise them. For example, right now, writing this chapter is allowing me to practise my writing and reflection skills.

When you find ways to use your strengths effectively, you'll feel alive and comfortable in your own skin. And as you continue to use them to help yourself and others each day you will see them grow exponentially. Happiness and joy are the result.

GLORIA TABI

Gloria is the author of *Inclusive Teams & Workplace: Everyone Wins!!*, the managing director at EVERYDAY INCLUSION and the founder of Voice Everyday Racism. Gloria's research specialises in social analysis on race, social inequalities and anti-racism. As a Black African-Australian woman, Gloria brings well-grounded knowledge and experience of the impacts presented in race and gender identities. With over thirty years of experience in project management, employment services, professional mentorship and business consulting, Gloria's ability to engage, negotiate and build worthwhile relationships across diversity, clients and demographics are her greatest skills. Gloria provides proactive, relevant and impactful training frameworks that are tailored to your business for a safe, productive and sustainable future.

Website: voiceeverydayracism.com & everydayinclusion.com.au
LinkedIn: gloriatabi & everyday-inclusion

HOW TO PUT THE ZEN BACK INTO YOUR ZONE

Jo Stevens

My goal is to live joyfully, to spread joy and to be the best version of myself.

Like most people, I have dealt with a lot of heartache in my life. In 1998, when I was seven months pregnant with my first child, I lost my mum to pancreatic cancer. As you can imagine, it was an extremely difficult time, and I don't think I dealt with the loss of my mother very well. I just packed up my feelings and got on with life, telling myself to be happy with what I had.

For many years, I did a great job hiding my feelings. I was constantly living on autopilot and putting my grief in a cupboard. I pretended I was okay, but I knew I wasn't. I was just good at hiding my emotions.

Fast-forward eighteen years, my life began to fall apart. My husband was diagnosed with post-traumatic stress disorder after serving twenty-seven years in the Australian Defence Force. To make things worse, later that year my dad passed away, and I crumbled into a mess.

I just didn't know who I was. I felt I was losing my identity.

Losing my dad brought back old wounds and the loss of my mum.

Growing up, I was a lot closer to my mum than my dad. She was my best friend, the person I could count on the most. When Mum died, Dad and I became closer; we were each other's support system. He was my connection to those memories, and we would talk for hours about Mum, which would make me feel safe and connected to my childhood. When Dad died, it was like losing my mum all over again. Without that safety net, my emotional insecurities were brought to the forefront of my relationship with my husband. We were in a very bad place, struggling to communicate and it looked as if our marriage was over.

During that time, I felt very unsure of myself – of who I was and where I was going. I was so unhappy and depressed that at times I felt as though my life wasn't worth living. My husband and I were constantly arguing. He was struggling with the transition from leaving the security of his job with the Defence Force, and I was struggling with the loss of my dad.

Life as a Defence wife was never easy. Our marriage was a constant roller-coaster ride, especially when you add in the unique stresses of military life. When you're married to a member of the Defence Force, you know firsthand the anxiety that deployments can bring, as well as the challenges of readjusting to life after a deployment.

My husband went on active service three times to Afghanistan between 2008 to 2012 with nine-month rotations. The long separations not only took a toll on his mental health, but on the mental health of myself and our two children. I often felt like the meat in the middle of a sandwich, caught between my children and my husband. Our parenting styles were very different, and when you add in the challenges of teenage years, it can cause a lot of mental anguish for everyone.

However, despite the challenges, I always knew our marriage was worth fighting for, and I realised we couldn't continue down such a destructive path. I decided to reach out and ask for help, attending counselling sessions. My husband was also getting the support he needed, and thankfully, we were able to work together on our marriage and discover, once again, the mutual trust and love that brought us together in the beginning.

We've been through some tough times, but we've always stuck together. To have a successful marriage takes communication, compromise and emotional awareness. It hasn't been easy, and it requires constant hard work. The one thing I realised was, as much as I wanted to blame my husband for everything that went wrong in our marriage, the truth was, I was carrying my own demons from the past and they were impacting my mental health, which therefore impacted our marriage and our family.

Once I knew our marriage was back on track, and my husband was getting the support he needed for his PTSD, I decided it was time for me to take back control of my own mental health. For so long, I'd been taking care of everyone else, I forgot to look after the most important person in my life – ME!

In 2018, I went on a personal development journey that I called 'the year of Jo'. I left my job as a teacher's aide in a special needs school and threw myself into counselling, workshops and retreats. It was during a retreat that I discovered mindfulness movements which I now call 'zen movements'. These breathing movement techniques literally changed my life.

Zen movements are a combination of qi gong, shaking yoga and mindfulness meditation. They provided me with a mindfulness tool I could use when I was feeling overwhelmed and helped to calm my anxiety in times of stress.

I'd been searching for something to support my physical and mental wellbeing, but had struggled with Pilates and yoga due to flexibility issues, and was so grateful to find something that did not require me to touch my toes or be in an uncomfortable position.

Zen movements are performed while standing. The slow, purposeful movements of qi gong allow you to slow down and calm the mind, while the shaking yoga helps you to shake off the inner dragon, the internal stress and overwhelm. Mindful meditation helps you to focus on the moment, allowing you to pause and reset. Within a few weeks of practicing the movements for myself, I realised I needed to share these techniques with others.

Becoming a zen mindful movement practitioner has been a privilege, and I love watching the transformation in my clients and how they, too, have utilised the techniques into their own lives to support their mental wellbeing.

Our mental wellbeing is just as important as our physical wellbeing, and having mindfulness tools to support us through times of stress is extremely important. For myself, having mindfulness tools has changed my life; they have provided me with a support system in difficult times.

In 2021, my mental health was once again tested when my two brothers passed away within twelve days of each other. Without the tools and the support network I had built around me, I am certain I would have fallen back into a deep depression.

My mental health is a journey, but I continue to live with hope, finding ways to bring more joy into my life and the lives of those around me. From my personal experience, I know how difficult it can be to cope with mental illness. It is my goal to highlight the importance of awareness of caring for your mental wellbeing, to find the right mindfulness tools that work for you, and to create a supportive network that can help you through your mental health journey.

What I've learnt about life is that it is way too short and we should live it to the fullest, spend quality time with the people we care about and live with joy in our hearts. We just never know what life is going to throw at us, and my hope is, that when my time comes to leave this world, people remember me with a smile and a moment when I brought joy into their lives.

TOP FIVE ZEN MINDFULNESS TOOLS TO SUPPORT YOUR MENTAL WELLBEING

Personally, I have found mindfulness tools to be a great support for my mental wellbeing. I believe we should all have our go-to mindfulness tools to support us when we are feeling stressed or overwhelmed.

What is mindfulness? Mindfulness is about being present in the moment and noticing your thoughts and feelings without judgement.

1. Mindfulness walking

A mindfulness walk has many wellbeing benefits, including reducing stress, improving mood and promoting brain health. A morning mindfulness walk is a regular mental wellbeing tool that I like to enjoy. It is the perfect way to start the day, as I love to feel the sun on face and the wind in my hair. I like to walk without any music or podcasts, as I've found it is a great way to be fully present and more aware of my surroundings. My morning walks help to clear the brain fog from sleeping, and I find my mind is more open and ready for the tasks ahead.

How to be mindful while walking:

- Pay attention to how your legs, feet and arms feel with each step.
- Focus on the sensation of your feet hitting the ground and the movement of your body as you move into your next step.
- Feel the wind on your skin and hear the sound of the birds singing. This can help you to forget your worries and clear your mind.

2. Mindfulness colouring

Colouring is one of my favourite mindfulness tools. I especially love doing it at night with some relaxing meditation music (no words), as it is a great way to wind down after a busy day. Focusing on the intricate patterns and filling in the blank spaces helps me to focus on the moment, and the repetitive motions involved in colouring help me to relax my mind, providing a much-needed respite from my racing thoughts.

How to be mindful while colouring:
- Feel the crayon or pencil on your paper. Allow yourself to become lost in thought.
- Think about what colours you are using and how they contrast one another beautifully.
- Turn off your thoughts, and allow yourself to be fully present.

3. Mindfulness laughter

There is nothing better than having a good laugh. It is a great mindfulness tool to reduce stress, and I have found that laughter is the perfect way to help get me out of a bad mood!

Laughter has helped me through some of the most difficult moments in my life, and as my dad would say, 'Humour through adversity.' A good laugh for no reason can make it easier to cope with difficult situations and is the best way to release tension and stress.

Hanging out with friends and having a good laugh is great for your mental wellbeing. It can help lift your spirits, let you forget about your worries and help you to focus on the good things in your life.

How to do mindfulness laughter:
- Take a few deep breaths in and out and observe a moment in silence.
- After a moment, start laughing. It may feel a little weird at first, but just continue with the process.
- Take a few more deep breaths and laugh again and gradually deepen the laughter.

A good laugh can increase your overall sense of wellbeing.

So go on … smile, laugh and live longer.

4. Gratitude

Gratitude has to be one of my favourite mindfulness tools. It has truly helped me during some of the most difficult times in my life. When I first started my mindfulness journey, gratitude was one of the tools I was first introduced to.

Each morning, I like to start my day with a simple gratitude process (see below) to remind myself to be present in the moment. This daily ritual has helped me to be more aware of the good things in my life – things I had taken for granted in the past.

At night, I like to journal about my day and reflect on my gratitude list and expand on my thoughts and feelings. Journalling has helped me learn to be more mindful, to be more self-aware and to focus on the positive things in my life.

Daily gratitude process:

- Forgive yourself for yesterday's mistakes. When we forgive ourselves, it allows room to move forward and live more fully today.
- Take in five long, deep breaths. Mindfulness breathing allows you to clear your mind and focus on the day ahead.
- Smile for no reason. When you smile at nothing in particular and with no reason, it releases endorphins which can help you to feel happier and more relaxed.
- Set your intentions for the day. How you start your day sets up the tone for how you will approach and interact with others.
- List five things you are grateful for. Write down things you are grateful for right now. Try not to overthink it, just write down the first things you think about. Remember, every day is a gift, and when we learn to be grateful for what we have, we are more open to new opportunities.

5. Zen mindfulness movements

My mental health is an ongoing condition, something I need to be mindful of every day. It's important to me that I have mindfulness tools to support myself when I start to feel overwhelmed. Zen movements is the perfect mindfulness tool to support my mental wellbeing.

Zen movements has helped to increase my self-awareness and has brought more peace and calmness into my life. The simple but effective breathing movements allow me to slow down my thoughts, bring my focus back to the present moment and allow me to pause and reset.

Zen movement breathing exercise:

- Sit on a chair with your feet flat on the ground, chest tall and your shoulders relaxed.
- Place your hands on your knees, and as you take a slow, deep breath in, raise your hands from your knees up towards your shoulders with your fingers relaxed facing down towards your knees.
- Concentrate on your breath and notice how it feels when you fill your lungs with air.
- On the out breath, place your palms outward and slowly exhale as you lower your hands to your knees.
- Concentrate on the exhale and notice how your body feels when you slowly release the air from your lungs.
- Continue this mindfulness breathing exercise three times, slowly raising your hands and taking a deep breath in through your nose, then slowly exhale through your mouth with your palms facing outward.
- Once you have finished your three zen movements, sit quietly for a few moments and let yourself pause and reset.

Thank you for taking the time to read my story, I truly hope that some of my mindfulness tips can help put the zen back into your zone!

JO STEVENS

Jo Stevens is the founder of The Zen Zone

Jo uses her expertise as a mindfulness and mindful movement coach to support clients' mental wellbeing with simple and effective mindful movement and breathing techniques that can help bring the stress levels down.

Jo is the coordinator of Common Grounds Networking Meetup. Common Grounds is a community of amazing and diverse business-women who come together to connect, laugh, share experiences, network and feel supported.

Jo, along with her good friend, Kirsty Fields from Social Ocean, are the co-hosts of Ladies Who Long Lunch. LWLL is all about building connections, catching up with old and new friends and encouraging women to take time out for themselves.

They provide business events with a dash of fun for:

- Ladies who need friendships and connections.
- Ladies who need to take time out of the business for themselves.
- Ladies who are looking to make genuine connections in business.

Jo is also a mother of two adult children and has been married for over twenty-five years. Jo enjoys spending time with her family and friends and is an advocate for mental health, believing that everyone should be mindful of their own mental wellbeing.

The Zen Zone was born from Jo's personal experience with mental health. Her husband was diagnosed with PTSD, and this put a huge strain on their family and most of all their relationship.

Sadly, Jo's own mental wellbeing was impacted as she was so focused on supporting her husband and being the strong one for her children that she neglected her own mental health. Jo was diagnosed with anxiety and depression and realised that in order for her to take care of her family, she had to take care of herself first!

Once Jo took control of her mental wellbeing, she was able to think more clearly, there was less friction in her house and she was able to be a more supportive wife and mother.

Jo believes that our mental wellbeing is just as important as our physical wellbeing, and her goal is to support others to keep themselves mentally strong through simple but effective movement and breathing techniques to help put the ZEN back into their Zones!

Website: jostevens.com.au & thezenzone.com.au

BE MINDFUL OF YOUR PERSPECTIVE OF BUSY

Karen McDermott

What do you think when you hear the word busy? Does it make you feel exhausted or energised?

There are two very different ways of looking at it, and we must be mindful to honour our perspective.

If we view the word 'busy' with a negative perspective we will have a negative experience, and similarly, if we have a positive perspective, we will have a positive experience. It's a scientific fact that we can't have both a negative and a positive thought at the same time! It's all about our perspective in life.

I believe that when we are busy doing what we love, we are energised by it; it fills us up more than it takes away. That's why I'm passionate about sharing the power we all have within to achieve the life of our dreams. Friends and colleagues, looking from the outside, often say to me, 'I know you're busy …' This happens more than I'd like to admit, and yes, I may be busy, but it's in a way that fills me up, because joy is a huge priority for me. I said goodbye to *hard busy* a long time ago and since then, I now live my best life, and that benefits others. Yes, I have worked hard through the years, but it never felt like work and it never *felt* busy because of the perspective I chose every day.

I now have a beautiful blend that allows me to be at home and present for my kids most of the time. I'm able to take them to school and pick them up, and I get to have fun with them in the school holidays. And that's what makes me happy.

When I think of *goodbye busy, hello happy*, I can clearly see the must-do and to-do lists we make for ourselves and how that can overwhelm us and steal our happiness. But when we change our perspective on what busy looks like for us, we can take control of the overwhelm. I'm a mum of six so I'm always going to be busy in some way or another, but when you're 'happy' busy, it's very different than being 'unhappy' busy. When I said goodbye to busy, I said goodbye to things that didn't raise me up; things that didn't fill my cup. I chose to stop 'doing' and start 'being' and that is where the key to a perfect blend resides.

I said goodbye to the things that pulled my vibration down. I said goodbye, or energetically blocked out, the people around me who were energy vampires. If we're honest, we all know people in our circle who are just out for themselves, and it's time to realise that they're giving themselves enough energy, they don't need any more from us!

Instead, I took back that time to spend with my children, because children are fun and re-energising. Many people have a different perspective on motherhood, and whatever you choose is okay, but I prioritise joy very highly, so I choose to have fun with my children. In my work, I always choose what brings me joy, which means I attract the most amazing clients. Joy is the filter I use to make my business decisions. Because I prioritise joy very highly in my life, when I choose what gives me joy, it's never going to feel like a chore. As the great Jack Canfield shares in *The Secret*, 'Joy attracts success, they go hand in hand, don't underestimate joy.'

As you are reading this chapter today, I hope you start to believe that you, too, *can* let go of the old conventional 'busy'; the busy that is a for-ever to-do list in your mind, always weighing you down, always calling to be ticked off. Perhaps you will ask yourself, *Am I going to change my perspective and choose happy busy instead?* Because we're humans, we like to have things to do, but sometimes we need to prioritise hanging out in our happy place more often. The power of the pause is very powerful and being zen could be doing the 'nothingness' we need to recharge. We can then accept the other times when we will be busy, especially in our minds, and that's okay, as long as we are choosing the right busy for us. And I will say it again: a 'busy' that recharges us as we go along is something we can enjoy doing!

Let's go back to the original idea that it's in our minds where we need to put the effort in, by choosing our perspective of what our definition of busy is. So take a moment and write down what your definition of busy is *right now*. And then, write down what you want your definition of busy to be. If your thoughts are around what you want it to be, you can start to declutter the busyness that weighs you down, that makes you feel heavy or doesn't make you jump out of bed in the morning. For me, I love to wake up excited to see what the day is going to bring. I believe it's important to have a dream and I like to plan three things every day that I can do towards achieving that dream.

So what changes can you see happening in your life that will take you from 'unhappy' busy to 'happy' busy?

Many years ago, I made a choice to say hello to happy. I'd been through a very dark period of post-traumatic stress and the wake-up call of having a double miscarriage was very harrowing and hard on my heart. But what I found in that time was that I had choices, and I chose not to worry about what other people thought of me. I could look myself in the eyes knowing I was living my best life, being true to myself. I wonder if those people who were having opinions of my life back then were able to do the same. From that moment of awakening, I have never looked back.

I stand true in the knowing that I am making the right choices for *my* life. I am living my passion and purposely striving forward with loving intention.

When I chose to prioritise joy in my life, I started to make decisions that were aligned with what I wanted and that was to experience life to its fullest. I wanted to find a passion and a purpose, and to make it happen. I wanted to help people, because that's what lifts me up. It makes me feel happy when I've made a difference in someone else's life.

So I invite you to write down ten things that bring you joy. Right now, in this moment. What does your list look like? Are they simple things that you can be grateful for *right now?* It's worth being aware that authentic gratitude is one of the fastest catalysts to attracting what you want in life.

We certainly don't need to go and do any extra educational courses to learn how to embrace them. Though it's possible we need to unlearn some of our teachings from the past, where we've been taught to believe we must sacrifice so much of ourselves for others. That's not what we need to do. Let's light ourselves up by finding our passions and our purpose to share with others. That's our gift with the world.

That's not sacrificing yourself; that's filling your cup as you go along because you're giving to others and to yourself. That's powerful. That's what we need more people doing in the world. And when you embrace that, you'll be saying goodbye to busy and hello to happy every single day.

And on those days when you're not feeling so happy or are a little overwhelmed, you can close over that to-do list and go for a walk on the beach or in the countryside. Get out in nature or just be with yourself, even blur on Netflix if that's what makes you happy. You can fill that cup and come back the next day and embrace the beauty of your purposeful work and your purpose for life.

My belief is that we're not supposed to have such a defined line between work and play. It's supposed to be a blend. And when you find your blend, you'll be in harmony with your heart, mind and soul.

That's when you make a difference in your life and inspire others to make a difference in theirs. 'Be the change you want to see in the world,' and everything else will ripple out from that.

So, say, 'Hello happy!' Make the choice from this day forward to choose and prioritise your happiness. When you make this choice, those around you benefit and others will be inspired by it.

In the words of the infamous John Lennon, 'Life is what happens while you are busy making other plans,' so whether you are doing or being in your life, keep a check on your 'busy' perspective, because there is so much more joy to experience when you prioritise what makes your heart sing. And that could be so fulfilling, you'll want to be 'busy' every day.

KAREN McDERMOTT

Karen is an award-winning publisher, author, TEDx speaker and advanced law of attraction practitioner.

Author of numerous books across many genres – fiction, motivational, children's and journals – she chooses to lead the way in her authorship generously sharing her philosophies through her writing.

Karen is also a sought-after speaker who shares her knowledge and wisdom on building publishing empires, establishing yourself as a successful author-publisher and book writing.

Having built a highly successful publishing business from scratch, signing major authors, writing over thirty books herself and establishing her own credible brand in the market, Karen has developed strategies and techniques based on tapping into the power of knowing to create your dreams.

Karen is a gifted teacher who inspires others to make magic happen in their lives through her seven life principles that have been integral in her success.

Website: serenitypress.org & kmdbooks.com & mmhpress.com

THE LIFE-CHANGING MAGIC OF LESS

Katy Garner

Many women start a business to get away from the long hours, stress and hectic life of their previous career. They're in search of a better lifestyle, with a desire to create a balanced and more enjoyable life, with time for family, more creativity and better flexibility to cope with the demands of motherhood. They dream about their ideal business and life and what this would look like, perhaps imagining days at the beach with their children, lunch dates with girlfriends, business trips to international destinations and fulfilling days running the business of their dreams. Unfortunately, for many women, this isn't the reality they create, and although they do now have flexibility, they end up working more hours for less return and never having time for their family, and certainly not time for themselves, or for fun!

They become burnt-out, overworked and begin resenting the business they had spent so long dreaming about, investing in and working on. How do we know this? Because this happened to us!

About two years into our journey, we found we had become crazy workaholics. We were working all day and late into the night! We were running a free online network with sixteen thousand members, a paid network with three hundred members, publishing two digital magazines every month plus a print magazine quarterly, holding conferences and events all over the country, exhibiting at baby expos, holding a national awards event, hosting online events, running, maintaining and promoting two blogs, running an online business directory – and because that wasn't enough, also working as publishers! On top of all of that, we were also looking after five young children at home.

We were working so much but had nothing to show for it! Our kids were unhappy, our husbands missed us and we were miserable. We found ourselves having the same conversation over and over again, and asking the question: 'Why isn't this working? We can't be doing enough. Let's do this as well and then maybe that will work!' I think the only reason we kept going was because there were two of us and we didn't want to let the other one down.

We felt completely overwhelmed by so much going on at once, and on top of this, Peace's son was accepted into the Australian Ballet School in Melbourne at just twelve years of age. This led to a major move to the other side of the country for Peace, and she also discovered she was pregnant with her fourth child.

We knew we couldn't keep going at the same pace; something had to give. We were faced with an impossible decision: we needed to either sell the business or walk away.

We found an interested buyer and very nearly sold the business, but the offer he made was insulting and his plans to bring in a marketing guru to redo the branding and pay him twice as much as he was offering us was the real deal-breaker.

We knew the business had potential. If only we could crack the code on how to make it work!

The first step was imagining how we wanted our life to look. We knew what we didn't want, so now we needed to focus on what we did want.

We realised that we could choose. And this was a powerful realisation.

We could choose to work fifteen hours a day or just one hour a day. We could choose to work at night and weekends, or to spend time with our family. We could choose to do everything ourselves or outsource things. We could choose to scroll social media in our spare time, or make time for exercise or going for a coffee with a friend.

We decided we needed to take a long hard look at what was going on and make some serious changes, because at the time, we were choosing to work way too much!

We had lots of extra little (and big) side projects that we simply didn't need to be doing. Some of them were too time-consuming, others didn't produce the results we wanted and others were just weighing us down. It was like spring cleaning. We went through everything, getting rid of as much as we could that we didn't need or want anymore, even shelving projects we still loved and 'might bring back later' but didn't have time for.

We then realised we had to 'let go' of the idea that we had to do everything ourselves and started to give more responsibility to our team.

This is one of the areas in business we struggled with – constantly pushing ourselves to do tasks that we hated and were not good at, and then spending hours creating projects that we loved but that made no money!

Mindset is often one of the biggest blocks to doing less. Maybe you've been told that to do well you have to work hard. Or perhaps you think you can do things better or faster than other people. You're scared if you automate everything, there'll be nothing for you to do. You believe it will be too expensive to outsource and you can save money by doing it yourself.

We LOVE what we do, of course we do, doesn't everyone? This isn't the problem. The problem is when your love becomes like an addiction. And being a workaholic is a lot like any other kind of addiction. Our culture just don't recognise it as one.

People say, 'The harder I work, the luckier I get.' Or, 'Hard work is its own reward.' People say, 'If you want to be successful, you have to work hard.' There's almost a badge of honour for those who work the 'hardest'. They pride themselves on it, and others comment on their good work ethic. But the truth is you don't have to work 'hard' to be successful or rich or happy. You do have to put in effort and take action and do the work, but it doesn't have to be 'hard', and it shouldn't be detrimental to your health or happiness.

The first thing you need to do is *stop* saying you're working *hard* or that you're *so busy.* Your mind believes what you tell it to believe, so if you can change your words, you can change your thoughts.

We had the mindset that we couldn't afford to pay others to do tasks for us, that they wouldn't be able to do it how we wanted and that it didn't matter how long things took because our time was free! This was a big mistake and actually stunted our business growth as we struggled along performing tasks like bookkeeping and Photoshop that would take us hours to complete. We should have been hiring experts to do it, who would have it done in a tenth of the time compared to the time we were wasting.

We were working in our zone of mediocrity instead of our zone of genius, wasting our time on tasks that should have been outsourced or weren't bringing in any profit.

We could all work MORE! Let's face it, there is always more we could be doing – more marketing, more social media, more press releases, more products, more campaigns. But no-one ever talks about how we can be doing less, or even that we *should* be doing less.

There's some sort of unspoken rule that says busyness is good and we all should be aiming to keep busy. But there's nothing glamorous about being a workaholic. And like any addiction, it can be detrimental to your health, your wellbeing, your family, and ironically, even your business.

If you are a workaholic, I don't want you to feel guilty or embarrassed or ashamed because we've been there. We know how hard it is to switch off and let go of work when you're working on an exciting new project or you've got an unhappy customer that's getting you down.

We have found, though, that by doing LESS, we were able to be more creative, more strategic and more productive.

It's not as simple as just doing less, though – you need to take the steps that will allow you to do less but achieve more.

It's a bit like motherhood. Your baby won't just instantly learn to walk. You need to provide the environment that gives them an opportunity to practise: an even surface, a safe environment, furniture to walk around on, positive coaching and encouragement, praise as they take their first step. And don't forget all the time you invested beforehand to teach them to crawl. Your business can learn to 'walk' independently too, but it's going to need the right conditions.

Our first step was to look at everything we were doing and understand whether we needed to be doing it all.

We knew there were tasks we were doing that weren't bringing in a decent return on investment. We were hanging on to some of them in the hope that, one day, they would. Others we were afraid to let go of and some we felt obliged to continue with because we'd already invested so much time and money into setting them up.

It's disappointing to let something go that you've poured your heart and soul into, but if it isn't working, you can't just keep pretending it is or doing the same thing and expecting a different result. One of the biggest lessons business has taught us is to listen to the market. If you bring a product or service to market and the market doesn't want it, or doesn't want to pay for it, you have to listen, pay attention and make changes. So often, business owners hang on to their ideas and projects for too long because they are passionate about them even when their customers aren't. If your customers are buying something else from you, that's an important piece of information about where to invest your time and energy.

Return on investment can be in the form of income, leads, sales, etc., but it needs to be something measurable. We found there were some activities and projects we were doing that cost us a lot in terms of resources, like time and energy, but brought little back in return by way of profit or targeted leads. Taking the time to really look at what was going on in our business meant we were able to identify these low-performing activities and make decisions on how to handle them.

You've probably heard of the eighty-twenty rule, also known as the Pareto principle. Pareto believed that 80% of your time is wasted on unimportant tasks and things that don't bring you much money, while 80% of your income is from 20% of the things you are doing!

He also believed that 80% of your customers aren't bringing you much money (and some never will) and that 20% of your customers generate 80% of your income.

Interestingly, 20% of your customers often create 80% of your problems too!

Imagine if you had the ability to remove that bottom 20% who were causing 80% of your problems.

Or, even better, if you had the ability to find out who the top 20% were that created 80% of your income and focus on them.

What if you were able to stop doing some of the 80% of things you were doing that only brought you 20% of your revenue and you were able to focus on the 20% of things that were the most valuable?

These were the questions we asked ourselves through this process. How do we create the best possible return on investment? How do we best use our time, attention and energy to create a more profitable business? How do we stop working ourselves into the ground, start working smarter and enjoy life again?

What would happen if we found the tasks giving us the best return on investment and just focused on them? What would our business look like then? How would we be spending our time?

What would we change if we were really focusing on the 20% of customers who meant the most to our business? Would we be doing things differently from how we were now?

This was a big moment for us; the realisation that if we were more strategic in how we invested our time and energy, we would be able to work less yet achieve more.

But how do you do that? Our first step was to write down everything we were doing in the business.

We had a LOT going on – we were trying to run two blogs, two websites, two sets of social media pages, two magazines, events, tradeshows, online education programs and advertising.

Yet despite all of the DOING, we were making almost no money.

We decided to get some big pieces of paper and map out everything we were doing. One page was for marketing, one page was for events, one page was for advertisers, one page was for the membership, one page was for the blogs, one page for the magazines, one page for the online education – and then we just got busy writing, listing every single thing we were doing.

Straightaway we knew which things we wanted to get rid of.

They were the annoying things that were just time-sappers and really didn't bring enough return on investment. We knew intuitively what these things were and that we shouldn't be doing them anymore, but we had a bad habit of hanging onto things that no longer served us.

An example of this for us was exhibiting at expos. They took so much time and energy in preparation, orchestration and then recovery after, as well as travelling and being away from our families. The results we were getting were nowhere near what they should have been for the energy and effort we put in, because the demographic wasn't the right one for us. It didn't make sense to keep doing it, and it was such a feeling of lightness and relief to let it go!

There were things we crossed off that we were happy to never do again. That was satisfying and instantly gave us back more time.

Next we looked at which projects we still loved but could shelve for a while. We shelved a lot of things, but a good example was our magazine. We loved the creativity of making magazines, and they did bring in some money, but they were time-consuming to produce. We knew that if we shelved these for a little while, no-one would mind and it wouldn't make that much of a difference to our business or profits. We also knew that we could do them again down the track if we wanted to, or for special occasions.

It was quite amazing how liberating it felt to simply give ourselves permission to take a break and stop doing these things for a while.

The next step was to look at what was left. This activity was so freeing, because once we decluttered all the junk, we found what really mattered! We realised that focusing on the things that mattered would make our business more valuable than running around doing busywork.

The sense of clarity we gained from this one exercise was amazing.

From here we could easily see what needed to be done and began creating simple one-page systems for the things we wanted to delegate out to our team of casual virtual assistants.

Our final step was to simply 'do what we love'. This activity allowed us to both completely step out of the business and take maternity leave when our babies were born, a year apart. When we did return, we were able to work just one hour a day and do whatever we wanted, knowing the systems and delegating we'd set up would keep things going in the business until we were ready to come back fully.

Designing a life that gives you back your time improves everything, and importantly, gives you the time you need to look after yourself properly. When you feel better, your business does better. People can tell. Your positive energy is contagious and they want to be around you.

Looking after yourself is also about finding time to do the things you enjoy. Reading a book, having a cup of tea, watching a TV show you like, cooking, crafts, catching up with friends for a coffee are all little things you can do to nourish your wellbeing. Something small every day, just for you, is important. If you need to organise someone to mind your children so you can do this occasionally, then don't be afraid to ask for help.

So there you have it, this is how we turned our lives around from busy to happy. We're both now happier, healthier and have better lifestyles than ever before. Our business is successful, fulfilling, rewarding and profitable, and we have time to spend with our families too.

Saying goodbye busy and hello happy is one of the best decisions we've made. What steps will you take to change your life?

KATY GARNER

Award-winning entrepreneur and author Katy Garner is the co-founder of Women Changing The World Press, The Women's Business School, AusMumpreneur and *The Best and Brightest* Podcast.

Katy's purpose is to support, educate and inspire women to create businesses that work for them. With a background in publishing, events and community engagement, she's passionate about being a voice for women and has been active in advocating for more recognition of the work of Australian women in business with local, state and federal politicians to encourage more funding and support for women in business. Katy has been on the board of the Queensland Small Business Advisory Council. Katy was awarded the QRRRWN Entrepreneurship Award in 2019.

For the past twelve years, Katy has organised the AusMumpreneur Awards, a national awards program that celebrates mothers in business and recognises the amazing achievements and economic contributions that mumpreneurs make to the Australian economy.

DANCING IN YOUR GIFT

Krystal Seang

To Vanna and Jade.
For dancing with me through life.

'When you dance, your purpose is not to get to a certain place on the floor. It's to enjoy each step along the way.'
Wayne Dyer

Can you remember the last time you danced? Can you recall the joy of being yourself, dancing one step to the next?

We live in a hustle culture that tells us we can *be*, *do* and *have it all*. We are fixated on getting to the next destination and addicted to being productive all the time. But unlike business or competitive sports, dance has no end goal except for the *enjoyment of the process* itself.

Instead of racing our way through life, how can we more fully enjoy the steps along the way?

Our modern economy offers us abundant opportunities to pursue our big dreams and reach our full potential, but as the pressures of 'adulting' stack up – mortgage, bills, kids – it's understandable if you're feeling the weight of the world on your shoulders.

Like many entrepreneurs, I chose the path of self-employment for passion and lifestyle freedom. But the fast pace of switching hats from mum, wife, business owner, cook and housekeeper can be exhausting. Left unchecked, a hectic work-life schedule for self-made success can lead to a mountain of overwhelm.

I first experienced burnout shortly after launching my startup, Tutornova, an online tutoring service, just months after giving birth to my daughter. I was committed to being the best mother and business leader I could be, but in reality, running a startup on bare bones capital while raising a baby took its toll financially, emotionally and physically.

Forget dancing through life ... I was tripping over my own feet!

What did I do? Like most, I pushed myself harder ... waking up earlier, sleeping later, drinking tons of coffee, working relentlessly when my baby was napping and pressing 'repeat'.

Despite my efforts, I constantly felt I was failing – both as a business owner and a mother. When I was working, I had a serious case of mum guilt and when I was being an attentive mum, I felt I was neglecting the business.

Persisting through months of exhaustion, the business was finally able to achieve product-market fit. The burnout phase eased when I began implementing business systems, automating processes and delegating tasks to a remote team of tutors and virtual assistants. This enabled the business to run smoothly without me working more hours.

I had achieved my finite goal of building a profitable, scalable subscription business that operated without me, for the most part. Though I was proud of what I'd built, the feeling of accomplishment was short-lived. I was no longer living in my strengths and talents, and lacked the passion needed to take the business to new heights. I missed the excitement of creative innovation and the satisfaction of teaching, but desired to work with a new audience of entrepreneurs. Disillusioned, I asked myself, *What now?*

That's the irony about achieving purely finite goals like possessions or dollar figures. The moment you 'arrive' at your destination, you lose your sense of purpose, and it is usually immediately replaced with a new condition for happiness. The key is to not limit your experience of happiness to the arrival of an end goal, but to enjoy the beauty of expressing your passions, values and gifts along the way.

I decided to sell the business. Looking back, I have no regrets. The lessons learned throughout my startup journey have led me to a more fulfilling, value-led approach to running a successful lifestyle business.

During this career pivot, life took a devastating turn. In late 2018, my beautiful husband and soulmate, Vanna, tragically died due to a sudden, unexpected illness. The love of my life was gone.

Life came to a standstill. Widowed at thirty with our one-year-old daughter, I fell into an existential crisis and began to question every social construct I'd dedicated my life to: what it meant to be a wife, mother, business leader and successful human. All of them seemed to fall away in the face of death.

I questioned everything I knew to be true, and asked myself, *What truly matters?*

My loved ones – my husband and daughter – and the moments we spent together.

My journey toward healing has been difficult and nonlinear. I learned to cope through self-compassion, relief in grief and finding solace in the distraction of seemingly unproductive tasks. What sustained me was the love for my husband and daughter.

I survived by taking life one day (or moment) at a time.

I learned the value of self-care as a means of survival, so I could get myself out of bed in the morning and take care of our daughter. It took relearning that achievements or social constructs did not define my true self or the strength of my relationships. Despite periods of anger and doubt, I found strength in God and the belief that we are all spirits having a human experience, living on borrowed time. Life is fragile, and all we have is *right now*.

In the life-changing book *Man's Search For Meaning* by Viktor Frankl, he wrote: 'Everything can be taken from a man but one thing: the last of the human freedoms – to choose one's attitude in any given set of circumstances, to choose one's own way.' After several years of living in survival mode, I wanted to choose a better life for us.

To not just survive, but thrive, it was up to me to make this change. These days, my goals revolve around my highest values: spending quality time with our daughter, nurturing her with love and life's amazing opportunities, and living in my gifts and talents. I still value lifestyle freedoms, like time flexibility, autonomy and financial independence, but the compass that guides me is *a love of the process.* It's not purely outcome oriented.

I still trip over my feet from time to time, slipping into an unsustainable hustle mode (usually over an exciting new project), but I'm getting better at pacing myself.

You don't have to learn lessons the hard way to shift your perspective. By living in your gifts and values – whether it's love, contribution, growth, creativity, freedom or peace – you have what it takes to design a life that feels meaningful, and thus brings you happiness.

My journey so far has led me to live by four principles for a fulfilling life, minus the burnout.

PRINCIPLE 1: START WITH VALUES, NOT OUTCOMES

Set career and personal goals based on your highest values, not outcomes, because it's the journey that counts. Arriving at your preset destination is never guaranteed. This way, you'll have no regrets about the journey.

In the book *The Top Five Regrets of the Dying* by Bronnie Ware, the most common regret amongst the dying was the wish that they had the courage to live a life true to themselves, and not the life others expected.

You are the master of the ship (your life). You might ask, *What is my destination?* but what if *there is no destination*, because happiness is not reached at the endpoint (your death).

You have a choice.

You can enjoy the wild ride of life in a spirit of hope, taking in the majestic views along the way, or if you so choose, you may steer the ship at full speed, eyes narrowed, wishing the whole experience was over.

Inevitably, you're going to hit rough waters where you may feel disorientated and pulled in multiple directions, because sometimes our values can clash with each other.

As a multipassionate entrepreneur, I love variety and enjoy taking calculated risks. However, I also value financial stability and free time for loved ones and hobbies. Saying 'yes' to *all* the shiny new objects can quickly lead to overwhelm.

To manage potentially conflicting values, regularly check in with your goals and action plans and ensure they serve all your highest values, not favouring one value at the expense of another.

Your turn:

What do I value?

What do I believe in?

What does a life lived 'true to myself' look like?

PRINCIPLE 2: LIVE IN YOUR TALENTS

'Identify your own gift because you already have it. Your gift is the thing you do the absolute best with the least amount of effort.'
Steve Harvey

Living in your gifts and talents is one way to experience happiness right now.

Gifts and talents are not confined to a traditional job title or craft, like athlete, artist, singer, actor or writer. You can also possess more than one gift. Gifts can take many unconventional forms!

For example, you may be a gifted teacher, but instead of teaching in a classroom, you are inspired to be an incredible role model for your children. Or perhaps you're a natural investigator who doesn't solve crimes, but innovates solutions to overcome problems within your niche industry.

If you aren't sure about your strengths and talents, consider completing a self-inventory activity such as the flower exercise from the career guide *What Color is Your Parachute?* by Richard Bolles, or a reputable strengths assessment such as the Gallup *StrengthsFinder*.

While knowing your values and talents is a strong starting point, you may not know what goals to set right away. These big life questions will unpack as you begin to take action.

Your turn:
What are my gifts and talents?
 What do I excel at with the least effort?
 What am I good at and enjoy doing?
 What career paths allow me to express my gifts fully?

PRINCIPLE 3: THE SELF-AUDIT

> *'You do not rise to the level of your goals.*
> *You fall to the level of your systems.'*
> **James Clear**

Many entrepreneurs choose self-employment for the freedom to work on their terms, but building a dream gig can be overwhelming, with so many moving parts and an endless to-do list. Unless it's a hobby, managing your finances and time is vital to staying in business.

While freedom may be the ultimate lifestyle goal, achieving this requires you to follow specific disciplines, known as the freedom-discipline paradox. Succeeding at the game of business requires understanding the rules of the game, adapting to changing market conditions and finding your competitive edge.

Such rules can take the form of business plans, systems, processes, habits, routines, workflows and checklists.

Following well-designed systems for recurring tasks will bring you (and your team) clarity of focus, accuracy and consistency, and frees up your headspace.

The following self-audit can help you prioritise your time and activities, so you can consistently live in your gifts and talents over the long run.

The Self-Audit:
Step 1: Brain dump
Write a list of all the tasks that fill your typical week. You may also include recurring monthly, quarterly and annual tasks.

Step 2: Sort
Now put those tasks into the following categories:
- *Delete* – Tasks that are not important or urgent. Timewasters. E.g. Checking emails hourly, excessively scrolling social media.
- *Delegate* – Tasks that can be outsourced to another person. Includes things you can't do, don't do well or don't like to do. E.g. Admin, accounting, cleaning.
- *Automate* – Tasks that can be turned into a system using technology. E.g. Recurring events in Google Calendar, meeting booking software, email automation.
- *Do it myself* – Tasks with the highest return on investment of your

time and energy. Applies your core competencies, gifts and talents. Includes planning and strategic work.

- *Maybe one day* – A holding place for future projects and ideas that you might come back to.

Step 3: Take action

Begin outsourcing tasks that will save you the most time and energy once implemented. While it takes extra time at the start to create systems and hire staff, delegating can save you countless hours in the future and even increase your earning potential, as you can focus on growing your business. Even if it may feel like an out-of-reach luxury, you can start somewhere and add to this over time.

Step 4: Repeat every three to six months

Your turn:

Complete your own self-audit.

PRINCIPLE 4: THRIVE IN REST

'Wherever you are, be there totally.'
Eckhart Tolle

We often bring so much passion, even obsession, in service of our goals that it can be difficult to take our foot off the accelerator. But forgetting to take time to rest and be present when we step out of the office can make us lose sight of what matters.

I don't believe a perfect work-life balance exists. Rather, we are in a constant dance between concentrated, short-term seasons of work and rest, oscillating between the extremes. The key is to not stay at either extreme for too long.

There is a time for focused work – to launch that project, write that book, finish that course – followed by a time for rest and recovery.

Taking time to pause and refill your cup is critical to your long-term success. Self-care means valuing your own needs, and this includes guilt-free rest, setting healthy boundaries and mustering the courage to say 'no' to requests that compromise your values.

Just like your talents, your form of self-care is unique to you, but should ultimately increase your physical, mental and spiritual reserves. Maybe you enjoy sipping on a cup of tea and zoning out to Netflix? Or prefer a screen break and going outside for a walk?

What are the greatest benefits of rest? Fewer illnesses, a sharper focus and the energy to show up as your *best self* when it counts most.

Be kind to yourself where you are now, as a perfectly imperfect human being, with no conditions attached. After all, we are human *beings*, not human *doings*.

Your turn:
List ten self-care activities that leave you feeling rested and re-energised. Schedule time into your weekly planner for both deep work and guilt-free rest.

You *can* pursue your bold dreams and live a life you love without working to your breaking point. You have the power to transform your life, say goodbye to the busy-for-the-sake-of-busy lifestyle, and say hello to a value-led, joyful existence.

Today, I invite you to live in your values and talents so that you can live a life that truly lights you up! None of us are guaranteed a tomorrow. Chase those big dreams of yours. Enjoy the process. Thrive in rest.

Dance your way through life.

KRYSTAL SEANG

Krystal is a business mentor and multipassionate entrepreneur who empowers business owners to create successful, purpose-led businesses doing work they love. She helps entrepreneurs experience greater clarity, fulfilment, joy and success in their work by living in their values, gifts and talents, while creating lifestyle freedom for themselves and their families.

Krystal brings over sixteen years of experience in small business ownership, specialising in strategy and planning, scalable online business models and systems design for consistent, sustainable growth. After building her edu-tech startup, Tutornova, and then selling the business in 2018, Krystal enjoys mentoring fellow entrepreneurs to grow profitable lifestyle businesses that prioritise time freedom, autonomy and financial independence.

Despite the pressures of our modern hustle culture, Krystal believes you can pursue your big dreams and live a life you love without working to your breaking point. She applies a practical, value-based approach and believes we can experience more meaning and joy when living in our strengths, gifts and talents, because dancing toward our goals is a more fulfilling and fun way to spend our time on this earth.

Krystal had the honour of judging at the AusMumpreneur Awards and teaching at The Women's Business School, which provides world-class education and support to female founders and business leaders. She was the recipient of the Gold Award for 'Digital Innovation' in the AusMumpreneur Awards 2018 for her work on Tutornova and was listed in Australia's Top 100 Coolest Company Awards 2013 by *Australian Anthill* for the business education video series, *The Entrepreneur's Tribe*. She holds a Bachelor of Laws and Bachelor of Business from the University of Technology, Sydney.

Krystal lives in Sydney with her daughter. When she isn't working, she enjoys relaxing with loved ones, coastal walks and cosying up with a good book.

Website: krystalseang.com

IF YOU WANT TO LEARN, YOU WILL

Kylie Ross

Being 'busy' and being seen to be busy was a badge of honour I proudly wore in my twenties. Having little sleep from working late (or partying) and starting again early the next morning was totally my choice, but there is only so much lack of sleep and poor diet your body can take before it says enough is enough. Then I became a first-time solo mother at forty-one years old and found a new kind of 'busy'. During these times in my life, I hit burnout from trying to do it all the expected way, and I knew I needed to find my way to move from busy to happy.

This is when my life really took a change, a change that I chose and was very intentional about. I moved away from all the busy hustle working for someone else, to happily working from my home office on what I chose to do. And it was especially important to me to be on call for my son.

This change in lifestyle began with me knowing what I wanted my life to look like and being mindful about the steps to get there. I didn't know how I was going to achieve it, but I knew I could *learn* what I needed to achieve it.

The motto I've lived and taught for many, many years helped me to get there.

If you want to learn, you will!

As a high school dropout I knew firsthand that *if I want to learn, I will*. My journey took me to university as a mature-age student (at the ripe old age of twenty-one) and I graduated with an accounting degree. As a lover of all things tech, I became a sought-after cost and systems accountant working in a few different countries throughout twenty-plus years of my career. I had what I thought I wanted, but it was forced into the work ethic of working long hours with no proper balance in my life. I'd worked hard for something I found did not make me happy and I was heading towards burnout for it too.

Following are the five steps I used to move from my insanely busy life to my happy, with a work-life balance I enjoy every day.

1. FIND WHAT BRINGS YOU JOY

Yes, we all need an income to clothe, feed and home ourselves. Sometimes that requires taking on some employment that just makes us more and more busy and less on the happy side. But while you work that job, never forget you have time to think and learn and plan.

As an IT consultant, I would travel anywhere from one to five hours most days in my commute to clients to work with them onsite. On my journeys, I would listen to podcasts that gave me information and insight into another world; the world where I was an entrepreneur and my own boss. A world where I didn't need to call my mom last-minute and have her cancel her plans to go and pick up my sick son from school because I was a three-hour drive away.

It was 2009 when I really put things in motion to get what I *really* wanted. I was working and living in Edinburgh for a finance company – think selling stocks and hedge funds. The Global Financial Crisis had recently hit – it was scary – and in one day, I lost a large amount of value on my city flat. All of our jobs were on wobbly ground. They offered pay cuts to our salaries or retrenchments. Not a fun situation to be in. After some thought, I ended up resigning and moving back home to Australia with my savings and a new plan.

Finding my joy was easy for me because I'd been dreaming about having a baby for years. It was completely scary and not the traditional way things are done, but I knew I didn't want to have a baby with just anybody. As I wasn't in a relationship, my plan was to use an anonymous donor.

Luckily, I fell pregnant quickly and began my journey of motherhood. This has been the happiest thing I have ever done and I reap the rewards every day. Of course, it was also the hardest thing I've ever done. Being a solo mum with an infant and still needing to work and fit into the corporate world, while experiencing a whole new level of exhaustion, was difficult to navigate, to say the least.

This first year of drop-offs and pick-ups from day care, while commuting daily to an office, gave me the determination I needed to start planning my own business. I also needed to work through the years of conditioning I had, believing you are only safe financially if you work for an employer. It was scary to contemplate thinking about working for myself, let alone actually making the change.

This is when I really began working on my mindset.

2. MINDSET IS KEY

If you can't visualise your new life, how can you achieve it? I knew I didn't want to work for others anymore or be tied to a nine-to-five onsite routine. As an IT consultant, I found it crazy to be required to be onsite when we could do everything from a laptop, from anywhere. However, with traditional ways of working, the employer needed to *see* you working for their own peace of mind. Today, the world is quite different, as we navigate the other side of the worldwide pandemic with more 'work from home' acceptance.

Planning how I would create my business to be everything I wanted began with meditation, journalling and a lot of visualisation. I had to be honest with myself about what I wanted my work day to look like. Not what I would say in a job interview to keep a potential employer happy, but what did I actually want?

I wanted to start my day after my son went to school and stop before he came home. I no longer wanted to work nights and weekends, as I wanted time to explore hobbies that interested me. I'd sacrificed a lot of what I enjoyed by working hard and being a mom. I'd never change that, but now, my son is nearly a teenager and his demands for my time are less. Suddenly, I can be me again. This was the most exciting part for me. To be ME again!

You can't make any significant changes in life without shifting your mindset. You have to *choose* to change and then follow through with intentional action to make this change happen. To actually transition into my new life, I realised I needed to keep my day job, but work fewer hours as a contractor, which would allow me time to build up a different side of the business. This is where knowing your worth comes into play. I needed to negotiate a better contract to work fewer hours for more money.

3. KNOW YOUR WORTH

For many years, I accepted what others said I was worth in my various jobs. It wasn't until I made friends with an HR consultant who told me the dollar amount I should be asking for with my skills and experience. I was also told to never accept the first offer in a negotiation. I took his advice and started asking for more money and more options throughout my career, and I began to receive what I felt I was worth. To know my worth made me happy. It also brings a new level of confidence, allowing you to ask for what you want.

As a new entrepreneur, I didn't realise what I didn't know, so I began learning everything I could. I'd love to tell you I succeeded quickly and started earning a six-figure salary the next week, but in reality it took me four business ideas and ten years of lessons learned to get where I am today. I'm an entrepreneur running an online business that provides mostly evergreen online courses and allows me to work 100% from home with time off as I need it. I love that there is no hassle anymore when my son has a sick day. He stays home and I continue with my day and monitor him as necessary. No more mum guilt of leaving my son when he's sick and needing me.

Again, we circle back to mindset shift. The biggest lesson when working for yourself is that you need to convince *yourself* what you are worth before you can convince anyone else. I did struggle with this at first and definitely offered my services and courses at a low price. Again, there is learning in all situations, and getting any sale is awesome. Once you know your product, course or service sells, you can then increase prices to suit.

Understanding your industry and rates is helpful, but at the end of the day, you are unique and the service you offer is unique, so charge what you are comfortable with is the best advice I can give here. I think we all start low when we first begin, but you'll surprise yourself at how quickly you start raising your rates when your confidence grows or you receive positive testimonials and have been working on your business for a period of time.

I recommend spending time on knowing your worth and what you want to achieve.

I can definitely say I am happy with our life now and being my own boss.

4. TIME BLOCKING AND TASK BATCHING

This is a tip I'm glad I found. Time blocking is where you block out time in your calendar for various tasks to give you time to deep dive into them. It's not just marking down all your to-dos, but allowing yourself time to action them in batches of same types of tasks.

Initially, I filled up my calendar with things to do and was never getting through them all and spending a lot of 'busywork' moving them to the next day and then moving all the next days' tasks and so on and so on.

Then I found what worked for me. I pick one task to deep dive into on a day and focus on that. This works well when you combine with the concept of 'batching'. Doing a lot of the same tasks together when you are in that process flow can save you a lot of time later.

In practical terms, this could look like working on your blog posts on Monday. You could batch write the first draft of, say, three to five blog posts (depending on the number of words you like to write). Writing a blog post could involve research as well as the writing part, but getting out the first draft is what I find the hardest part. You can then edit something you have drafted, but you can't edit what you haven't written.

Then on Tuesday you can create the image(s) for your posts and edit them. This works really well, I find, with creating my YouTube videos and online course videos. I create the draft videos one after the other for the time I've blocked out. Then, in the next session, I work on editing them. It's much easier to rinse and repeat similar tasks in a batch than to work end to end on a single video and then start again.

This was one of the best tips I've used in my entrepreneur journey to move me from busy to happy, because I feel like I'm actually achieving and completing tasks, rather than looking at a never-ending and always growing, long list of to-dos. It's addictive and gives you confidence when you see yourself finishing task after task.

5. AUTOMATE MANUAL TASKS & STREAMLINE PROCESSES

Running your own business can be extremely time-consuming, especially in the early years as you work all hours building your business. For me, I found the busywork and repetitive tasks were taking up too much of my time, when I could be serving my clients and working on new online courses, video tips and other resources.

Traditionally, I would list my daily tasks in my paper calendar or notebook. I'd tick them off as I completed them and then rewrite the list for the next day. Wow, even typing how I used to organise my work exhausts me. Being a lover of tech since my first PalmPilot, I knew I needed to stop working the traditional way and find new ways that suited the way I like to work, to automate my repetitive and busywork tasks. Learning this is what has now evolved into my online business. I realised if I wanted to work differently and more efficiently, so would many other working mums and entrepreneurs, especially those who didn't grow up with tech.

This epiphany is now my online business – teaching online business owners how to use the tech tools they need to run their business. I also teach how to be tech confident and utilise apps to make your life more automated and streamlined.

I have an app for recording all my projects and to-dos and this allows me to set reminders, checklists and automate moving the task from one list to another depending on the status rules I've set. If I didn't have this app, I'd be relying on my memory, and these days, it doesn't work as fast as it used to. So I rely on my tech tools to help me out and remember for me.

Another great automation I have is a calendar booking app that integrates with my website. Potential clients can book a one-to-one coaching package with me, pay for it and book it into my calendar without me being involved at all. The booking then triggers a to-do in my project management tool, depending on the type of coaching package it is, and includes a reminder for me to prep for the session and add the relevant checklist of items to the task. Additionally, this booking also adds the appointment to my main calendar to allow me to plan my day, week and month easily and quickly.

Figuring out which apps and tech tools you need can be very

confusing and frustrating, especially if you are of a generation that did not grow up with tech. I was a teenager in the eighties and we didn't have devices or even remote controls for the TV. Automating our lives was not a term we even considered, but what I've learned over thirty-plus years as an accountant and teaching software in the corporate and small business world is that:

If you want to learn, you will!

You learnt how to walk, talk, read and write. If you want to learn to be more tech confident, you just need to want to, and you will!

KYLIE ROSS

Kylie Ross is a creative entrepreneur with a passion to help other entrepreneurs, content creators and writers be their best tech-savvy and tech-confident selves.

Kylie is a retired accountant and IT consultant with over thirty years in the corporate and small business world implementing, consulting and teaching users how to use their software. She has lived and worked in various countries over the last twenty years and thoroughly enjoyed meeting an amazing range of people, experiencing different cultures, working in a range of industries and receiving the unofficial title of 'tech translator'.

Being a teenager in the eighties and not growing up with tech or using it at school, Kylie is well aware of how hard it can be for others with similar experiences to pick up today's apps, software and tech. Then one day she was asked by a client, 'What is the cloud?' The creation of an explainer video sparked the idea to create Tech Savvy Creatives and the Tech Savvy Toolkit websites which contain a range of DIY online courses and one-to-one coaching programs designed to help others become proficient with popular software to run their business, streamline their processes and create automations to enable them to scale and grow their own business with ease.

Kylie's motto, *If you want to learn, you will!* is very true, and she has many happy students and clients who are now more tech savvy and tech confident because they wanted to learn.

Kylie now lives in her hometown of Brisbane with her son and fur babies and enjoys a travel-free lifestyle working from her home office and hopes to draw her focus away from helping other entrepreneurs, writers and creatives with the tech tools they need long enough to actually complete a fiction series she has been working on for more years than is comfortable to say.

Website: techsavvycreatives.com & techsavvytoolkit.com

PACKING UNDIES

Lesley Webster

If you are reading this, then you may relate to where I've been. Too busy and pretty unhappy. When I began writing this chapter, I looked up the definition of happy – *feeling or showing pleasure or contentment*. Let's break that down. Think about the last time you felt pleasure, showed pleasure, felt happy. When was the last time you thought, *I am content with what I have? I have enough. I am enough.* Take a deep breath.

Then I looked at the definition of busy – *having a great deal to do*. Well, like a lot of people, I am a mother, wife, business owner, colleague, daughter, sister, friend, confidante, daughter in law, etc. etc. etc. etc. (And not necessarily in that order on any given day!) My relationship list went on and on and so did my list of things to do!

Personally, I use an app for my to-do list (even the terminology makes me shudder) and it had 186 tasks on it at some point (only once did I venture to look at the to-do counter). Let's be realistic here, by the time I could read the list through, I had wasted half a morning and made (and consumed) copious cups of coffee by way of procrastination.

What kind of tasks were on there? From grocery shopping lists to organising social events, birthday gifts and parties to attend, Christmas ideas, updating passports, appointments, selling stuff, school stuff, paying bills, cancelling things, applying for things, fixing things, reviewing things – do people actually shop around for the best insurance quote or do we stay where we are and put up with the ridiculous higher payment? Oh, and launching a business with my husband while working full-time with two children immediately prior to a pandemic. *Hmmmmm, take a breath, Lesley.*

Reflecting on it as I write this, I see now the first sign was that an element of confusion had set in. I was forgetting things, not concentrating and not present with the people I loved and cared for. I had aches and pains in places I didn't know I had places. I was exhausted but couldn't sleep and had trouble focusing on the simplest of tasks. Procrastination became an art because my head was so busy, I couldn't focus on one thing. This busy life was already too much pre-pandemic – something I hadn't realised – and the pandemic just exacerbated and highlighted the fact my to-do (*eeuurgh* and shudder) list was simply unachievable. It upped the stress ante several notches every time I thought about it.

Turns out, I was not alone. Once I had built up the courage to tell people and be open and present that I was not in a good place, some people secretly admitted they were in the same boat. Maybe not exactly in the same boat, but certainly on the same journey. I say secretly because personally I felt when I mentioned my mental health with some acquaintances, there was immediately a stigma, sympathy not empathy, and let's face it, when someone thinks someone is drowning, initial thoughts can be how easy it would be to climb on top of them to get air and take a breath. Don't get too close in case it's catching. Or is it because, like an addict, we cannot say things aloud because it makes it true? It can be confronting. People don't know what to say to you and I didn't want them to feel uncomfortable. This is a clue to a common theme amongst humans – how you make other people feel around you and your concern around not upsetting them often places your needs last.

Because so many people were on this same journey, I felt selfish talking about myself. We were all on the same boat, were we not? Why was my story any different to anyone else's? Surely I can't moan about things if we're all going through the same issues? Luckily for me, I have some amazing family, friends and colleagues and have built a network of support in Australia and in the UK that has stood the test of time, and without them, well, things would be vastly different.

This circus juggling act had been my life, on reflection, forever. I suspect I have always been busy. I swallowed books as a child and beyond, and lived my entire life in them, going on long journeys so I wouldn't be lonely in my real life. I read, I wrote, I found things to do, and this included helping other people as much as possible – yes, I was the habitual volunteer. At one event, I was jokingly asked by my husband not to volunteer – we already had too much on – but I just couldn't help myself, much to everyone's amusement. I felt guilty if I had to let someone down because I couldn't fulfil a commitment. This was the same in my career.

I realised I needed time on my own, for reflection, something I didn't even know I needed. I actually didn't know how to do this. No-one had advised me this was a thing. Having the ability to reflect is a learned skill, and believe me, I'm still learning. It helps me move forward and gain insight into things. I can problem-solve and make decisions, and some things I reflect on are positive, while some, not so much. I want to be able to reflect on things so I can eventually pack them away. I am not going to overpack the case, though. What if it breaks open and my undies go everywhere? So, I reflect in small doses. If you pack everything away in one go, one day the case will break open and your undies will be all over the place.

I was fostered as a baby. This led to me growing up in an environment with much older siblings who were already an established family.

Family made me evolve and moulded me to fit in. I often felt lonely, so I kept myself busy. My siblings were busy adulting, and although they are really wonderful humans, being fostered and eventually adopted at fifteen brings its own set of challenges, which are not for this chapter.

There is a term for someone who goes out of their way to help others: 'people-pleaser'. I thought I was just being kind and helpful, but as I have learned, like everything in life, it goes much deeper than that. It can also relate to low self-esteem and trying to fit in – approval, acceptance, belonging. The joy of being needed, being enough.

It takes a long time to learn about your foibles. Sometimes they are hard to admit, but it is what makes us all different and all human. The trick is to be aware of them and aim to accept them because you are you and you deserve to live the life you want to live.

Being originally from the UK, most of my career happened there. I was a highly successful regional manager with, at the time, the largest financial services broker in the UK. I encountered a line manager there who is, still to this day, one of the best managers I have ever worked with, opening my eyes to *personality types*. I was immediately fascinated. I studied mine in detail – the good and the bad, the strengths and the weaknesses – and also found that this particular testing allowed for variation due to their scaling method. I wasn't placed into a box merely identifying personality type, strengths and preferences, but as it turned out, it is possible to be in-between personality types. I was also informed that I have such a vivid imagination, I may start more projects than is humanly possible to finish! It was pretty accurate, so how can I stop being so busy when I am actively absorbing people's needs and wants, as well as seeking out new tasks to do? I was basically at war with my own demands.

I know now it was only a matter of time before I hit burnout, and my husband, besties and a couple of work colleagues clicked first and showed obvious concern. Probably before I did. I soon recognised I was clearly not myself. I felt tired and lacklustre, with little joy in my life. I started talking about it. Reflecting on it. Researching it (in true personality type style) and knew I had to make changes. And fast.

Previously (to my light-bulb/meltdown moment), I just would not risk standing up for myself when it came to my time. I had let other things and people rule my life. Yes, we all have commitments we need to keep, but do the kids need to do ten different extracurricular activities every week? Slight exaggeration, but I know you hear me. Do we need to push our children so hard academically or can we relax that slightly? Do we need to run the kids party like the Oscars? Do we need to maintain a show to people – mostly acquaintances – that we can run everything with no cracks appearing? *Keeping Up With the Joneses* has never been so rife or damaging to our mental health.

I recognised there were people who cared about me. I needed to be present for my children and partner. When children are growing, these are years you never get back. That's when I started thinking about demands versus lifestyle. And my husband and I made a huge decision together: 2022 would be our year of risk.

I hear you ask, *Year of risk? Whoaaa.* Yes, risk.

Let's look at all the risks you've taken in your life. Some good, some bad, some you probably can't even remember. What does a risk look like to you? To me, with a financial services background, I relate it back to investments, to being risk averse or risk seeking (I prefer the word adventurous – sounds much more fun!).

I took a massive risk coming to Australia in 2010 and leaving a lifetime behind. My husband and I took a massive risk in 2019 ploughing all our time and money into a business venture – pretty risky, no? If we think about it, we take daily risks. A friend sent me a meme recently that said, *Adulthood is like looking both ways before you cross the street and then getting hit by an airplane.* It is little wonder we absorb stress as a daily way of life when we have all these adult responsibilities!

We are all excellent problem-solvers, we just don't give ourselves enough credit. I often give myself a pat on the back now just for solving the simplest of tasks! I find a quiet spot for five minutes first thing in the morning and set out to achieve one goal (and take a deep breath). It might be to do the shopping, read a chapter of a book or even call someone. I am trying to call more people, so I can hear their voice and their emotion. I have observed that I'm not always honest in messages. I can sound cheerful when I am not, and I wonder if other people could be the same, so speaking is particularly important. Whatever the task, I can confidently say I achieved it at the end of the day.

I have worked out I want to be a bit more adventurous and take some more chances to achieve my goals. And as long as I don't harm anyone along the way, then what can possibly go wrong? Actions have consequences and the consequences are not always bad, sometimes they can be excellent! So which type are you? Or which one did you used to be? (Very important to reflect on any pre-partner, pre-kids, pre-colleague you!)

I worked on achieving less (yes, less!) and congratulating myself more by scaling down the dreaded to-do list, gradually using three columns. Needs to be done = immediate; can be done soonish = future; and bin = no explanation required – it is empowering and my favourite column. I only allow twelve things on there at a time which forced me to explain to people that I cannot attend that event, complete that assignment in that timescale, put my needs last or absorb any negative energy. No is an enormously powerful word that should be used wisely and firmly and often requires no justification. I have heard people explain they cannot attend something and go into detail about why. You don't need to do this. Unless you want to, of course! *Sorry, I can't make that date/event,* should suffice.

Finally, I am not a fan of the term 'midlife crisis'. I feel reaching certain milestones is more of a 'life sign' to inspire you to live, to believe that life is for living, and please believe me when I say you can start that at any age, because ageism is discrimination, and we just can't have that.

Work out what you really enjoy doing and set boundaries for you and the people in your life. Be present in the moment and take a risk, however mild. Learn how to say no, and learn to reflect and pack things away in undies sizes.

And ditch the list.

Now go and enjoy that life you have there.

LESLEY WEBSTER

Lesley is a versatile operations management professional with extensive transferable skills gained in varied industries from the UK and Australia. With strengths in business operations, HR, finance, sales/marketing and business development, she is highly organised with an exceptional level of attention to detail and great interpersonal and problem-solving skills.

Lesley and her partner Joe have two businesses under the Launch Drinks umbrella: Pops by Launch, an award-winning, highly successful frozen gelato brand and Altobelli 1951, a classic, fine beverage collection.

The concept of alcoholic sorbet pops was born in a 'eureka' moment one evening when Lesley and Joe couldn't decide between an alcoholic drink or a dessert. After much deliberation they thought, *Porque no los dos?* – why not have both? Having your own business, working another full-time job and having two young children is a tough gig, never mind launching a new innovative product a few months before a pandemic! In light of this, Lesley recognised that it was more important than ever to share the love and joy that cocktail sorbet pops can bring to people during this new normal. After several taste trials (very hard work!)

months of licensing, applications and copious amounts of paperwork, they eventually began crafting their pops.

No-one else had created a sorbet product like this, and the joys of being able to be creative with the design, sharing a love of everything art deco and experimenting with daring flavours, was absolutely thrilling! There was a compelling need to 'just go for it' – to be able to work without parameters except for the ones you set for yourself, there is really no freedom like it. The product came with challenges, delivery logistics being one, but these challenges were eventually overcome through sheer determination and reverting to the drawing board on several occasions! Pops by Launch has proven so popular, five new flavours and designs have been added to the portfolio.

The Altobelli 1951 brand was inspired by classically passionate Italian vibes from Joe's culture with a design twist of eighth century Viking Scandinavian Scotland from Lesley's culture. The collection includes aperitifs and digestifs, like aperitivo, limoncello and amaro, and ready-to-drink cocktails, like negroni and dirty gin.

There are many benefits to balancing business and motherhood as Lesley explains, 'The work-life balance is a real bonus and having freedom to plan your day around what suits you is a major plus. The word entrepreneur by its very definition is about taking risks, and I hope that my children will chase their dreams as I have done and have the courage and resilience to believe in themselves – I can only hope that I have shown them this by example.'

It can be challenging to be a successful business owner whilst raising a family, and Lesley gives this advice for others thinking about starting their own enterprise: 'My advice for people with a great idea looking to start a business is don't be scared, don't be afraid to ask for help and show vulnerability. Display your passion by giving your customers a service they will never forget and learn from all feedback whether it be negative or positive and strive to enjoy the ride!'

Website: popsbylaunch.com.au & altobelli1951.com.au
Phone: +61 449 668 566
Email: info@popsbylaunch.com

ACCEPTING IMPERFECTION

Margaret Foley

My desire to be perfect at everything I did in my life was all consuming and I didn't even realise it existed. My need for perfection had been there my entire life, and I knew no other way to be. I can laugh about it now and call myself a 'recovering perfectionist', but my story of how my obsession with being perfect nearly cost me everything and how I recovered is one that I hope will inspire you in your life. I will also share with you my seven steps to living a life you love and finding your happy.

Perfectionism led me to burnout, anxiety, depression, high blood pressure and a host of other conditions. Self-worth and self-love were absent from my life. I felt lost, angry, sad and alone, yet if you asked one of my colleagues or a friend, they would tell you I was happy, positive, energetic and inspiring. On the inside, I was a scared little girl desperately seeking love and approval and doing whatever it took to get it. It's important that I tell you a little of my story to help you understand how connected the child is to the imperfect adult.

I had a private school education, adventurous holidays and a middle-class upbringing, however, I was realising as a young child that

I felt emotions more deeply than most others, but I was labelled as too sensitive and told to get over things and toughen up. The term 'empath' didn't exist back then. I was just called 'soft' instead.

Again and again, I would strive to gain the approval and love of my parents, to make them proud of me. I was a bright student at school but ninety-five out of one hundred on a spelling test was met with, 'What happened to the other five?' I tried so many ways over the years to gain my parents' approval, but it felt like it never came.

As I moved into adulthood, I embarked on different career paths before falling into sales. It saw it as the perfect career for me – my worth could be measured in the achievement of sales targets and the accolades and recognition that would follow. I was a gifted communicator, a fast learner and an insightful reader of human needs – all good talents for a high-performing salesperson. I threw myself into my career with gusto, feeling that, at last, I was approved of and worthy, not realising that this was temporary and external and wouldn't bring me the deep happiness I craved.

Motherhood took me to a deep level of anxiety – how could I be the perfect mother and raise perfect children? I became obsessed with getting every detail right and worried about what people would think of me. My first experience with depression came in the form of postnatal depression after the birth of my first son, which was further compounded by a miscarriage only a few months later. All my suppressed feelings of shame and inadequacy came rushing to the surface – I was a failure as a mother, as a wife, as a woman. I saw my miscarriage as a sign that I was faulty in some way and my depression as a sign that I was weak and flawed. And if I was those things, then I couldn't possibly be loved *by anyone.*

It was my first conscious awareness that I had drawn a straight line between being perfect and being loved: if I am not perfect, then I am not worthy of being loved. I connected invisible dots all the way back to my earliest days of not being good enough, not being loved enough, of being rejected, of being shamed, and the spiral of perfectionism began.

I've been married – twice. My first marriage brought me two sons who are my greatest joy. My second marriage brought me important life lessons. I had always dreamt of my Prince Charming treating me like a precious gem. Even when my prince didn't appear and I didn't get spoiled as I had imagined I would be, I accepted it. I didn't want to be a fuss, a bother. What I was really saying to myself is, *You don't deserve those things. You aren't worthy of anything special.* I would try a little harder to be a little more perfect, all to no avail, which only served to deepen the wound a little more. At the end of both marriages, I felt I had given all I could, and I still wasn't enough for them. And so, my narrative was reinforced.

Now I was a single mother with a burgeoning career and no-one to tell me I was too much or not enough anymore. I threw myself into my career, unshackled from worrying about what anyone thought. I could be whatever the hell I wanted to be. My career and motherhood were my focus, but my motivation was askew. I often said these words: 'My career is the one thing I haven't managed to screw up, so I'm going to focus on that.'

Over a period of a decade, I worked hard, connected with the right people and progressed to a senior role. Here's where the busy part really went off the charts. I was routinely working a sixty-hour week. When I was home, I was busy keeping my household running, supporting my then-teenage children through school and their own mental health battles and making time for my relationship. I tried to be perfect at everything, worrying that I would be judged and found lacking by my children, my friends, my employer, my partner. I put so much pressure on myself to keep striving and keep doing, being and having more.

Even when I did have some downtime, I felt I couldn't stop and rest. There was no 'me time'. I needed to always be busy, always doing some-thing, because the more I did, the more I proved myself as capable and worthy and the more approval and love I would receive. I was addicted to being busy, I was addicted to the high that I got when my boss praised me, when I smashed that target, when my kids achieved in their sport. *Busy = money + possessions = happiness,* or so I thought.

Eventually, busy turned into stress which then morphed assiduously into burnout. I now had everything I thought I had ever wanted, yet I was more unhappy and unhealthy than I had ever been. Being busy found me in hospital for the third time in five years, thinking I was having a heart attack. Busyness gifted me with digestive issues, hormonal disregulation, adrenal fatigue and an overwrought nervous system.

Here I was, at forty-nine years old, with the realisation it was time to get serious and make changes in my life. I engaged a life coach, a spiritual coach and worked with a psychotherapist to heal my past traumas. I listened to the nagging sense of discontent that was bubbling inside me, telling me that everything I needed to be happy was already inside of me, if only I could stop being busy and be quiet and listen instead.

Time spent in nature grounded me and helped me learn to be present. I spent hours sitting in the sunshine journalling my thoughts, answering my own questions and reading a small library of books which only raised more questions. A pivotal moment was connecting with and listening to my inner child through meditation, as she taught me to give to myself the love and approval I had been seeking from others. I learnt to accept and surrender my past, offering forgiveness to those who I believed had wronged me and forgiving myself for what I did when I did not know better.

Many tears were shed as I started to develop true self-love, with my awakening into finally knowing unconditional self-love opening my eyes to how much love I already had in my life. One by one my health issues began to resolve, as I found myself rested and healthy for the first time in years. The relief was palpable as the fog cleared and my future became clear. Once dreamt, the dream couldn't be unseen. Once felt, the calling couldn't be ignored. My eyes and heart were opened to know that my purpose was to live a life I love and help others to do the same. I resigned from my job and ventured out to support women transform their lives.

I was supported on this journey by some loving family and friends who, despite me thinking I had done a great job of pretending to be someone else, saw the real me. To be seen and affirmed isn't needed when you are centred in yourself, yet to be told by my partner 'I've always seen you' was a powerful validation of my imperfect perfection.

From my own healing and transformation, I have identified seven steps to finding happiness and living a life you love.

1. GET CLEAR ABOUT WHAT YOU DON'T WANT TO HAVE IN YOUR LIFE

Don't think about how you'll make changes or how realistic something is – just write a big, long list of all the stuff in your life you wish you could get rid of.

- What emotions are draining you? Are you stressed, anxious, tired, angry, sad, resentful?
- What people or situations are bringing you stress or unhappiness? Is your workplace toxic? Is your relationship unhealthy?
- How do you feel about yourself? Do you doubt yourself and lack confidence? Do you look in the mirror and not like your reflection?

2. START IMAGINING WHAT YOU DO WANT INSTEAD

It may be challenging to do this initially, try using your 'don't' list and think of what the opposite of that is.

- How do you want to feel? How do you want your health to be? Who or what do you see when you imagine a life that you love?
- If you were not stressed and anxious, what would you be instead? If you could overcome being busy and overwhelmed, what would that look like?
- Write this list and then read it daily, pausing to breathe in, visualise and feel into it. Imagine yourself being calm and peaceful, see

yourself being happy with your body – breathe in, sigh it out and feel the weight lift just a little each time.

3. MINDSET IS EVERYTHING

Pay attention to how you talk to yourself, the words you use when reacting to people and situations. You cannot control many things in life, but you can control your reactions, your thoughts and self-dialogue.

- Do you catastrophise when things don't go according to plan? Do you expect the worst and feel affirmed when it happens? Do you find yourself saying things you heard your parents say?
- Write down the things you find yourself saying and then create alternatives that you could say instead. For example, instead of saying, 'Once again, nothing works out for me,' try saying, 'That didn't quite go the way I would have hoped, and that's okay.'

4. INTRODUCE MINDFULNESS INTO YOUR DAY

This is a critical practice to adopt.

- Start with short, guided meditations of three to five minutes. Don't worry if your mind wanders away, notice it and then return to listening again. Your mind is a muscle that needs exercising to get stronger and then you will find yourself able to meditate for longer.
- Breathe. Deep breathing has many benefits for mental and physical health, the most important being the connection to the vagus nerve which acts to slow the heart rate and calm the digestive system. Even just thirty seconds of deep breathing will help calm you, a daily practice of two to three minutes will have noticeable benefits to your health. My favourite is simple box breathing. Breathe in through your nose for a count of four, feeling your belly rise as you fill your lungs with air. Hold the breath for the count of four. Breathe out in a sigh or *haaaa* sound through the mouth for the count of four. Pause at the bottom of the exhale for four counts and then repeat.

- Spend time in nature – it will recharge your energy. Journal your thoughts and feelings and get it all out.

5. GET TO KNOW YOUR INNER CHILD

Little YOU holds the secrets to your happiness.

- Guided meditation is the most effective way to reach them. Listen to them, nurture them, connect with them frequently and love on them hard.
- Your inner child will show you the real you. They will remind you how to be playful, they will show you deep unconditional self-love and much more.
- Notice how you talk to your inner child with kindness and compassion. Then start talking to your adult self in the same way and watch what happens!

6. LEARN AND LIVE IN ALIGNMENT WITH YOUR VALUES

So much resentment and lost energy comes when you are not living in alignment. When what you think, say and do are aligned, you find happiness. Too often we think one thing and say another, or we say one thing and do differently, because we are either afraid of what others might say or we don't trust our intuition.

- Complete a values evaluation exercise and come up with just three core values that will guide how you live your life. This is also a great activity to do with your family, especially children.
- My values are love, honesty and respect. I always lead with love, I am honest with myself and others and I have respect for myself and others. If I am feeling wobbly or uncertain, I ask myself whether what I am doing or considering doing is aligned with my values, and often it is not, then I can realign and come back to my heart again.

7. CONNECTION IS CRITICAL

We aren't meant to do life alone. Notice the people with whom you feel your energy lift – those are your people.

- Join groups online or in person such as women's circles, walking groups or volunteer organisations.
- Engage in a new course or study – reignite your mind and learn alongside others with similar interests especially in self-development and spiritual fields.

You don't need to always be busy and achieving to be worthy. You always have been and you always will be enough – just as you are. Perfectly imperfect.

MARGARET FOLEY

Margaret lives on the Mornington Peninsula in Victoria, Australia, with her two sons, two cats and a dog. At age forty-nine, Margaret experienced physical, mental and emotional burnout and as part of her recovery from this explored many traditional and non-traditional healing and therapeutic modalities, but nothing truly resonated. She turned inwards to herself, choosing instead to pay attention to the voice inside which was telling her that everything she needed to be well and happy was already within her. Connection to self, her inner child and her inner goddess through meditation and mindfulness, combined with working with a life coach and psychotherapist, Margaret came to know her true purpose in life was to work in the service of others, helping them to connect to their true self and live a life they love.

In 2021, Margaret resigned from her $250,000 a year job as a senior vice-president in a software company and founded Queen of my Own Universe, a life and mindset coaching business for women. Through Queen of my Own Universe, Margaret works with women seeking guidance to overcome trauma, abuse, burnout and dissatisfaction with their life. Every woman can be the queen of her own universe when she truly knows herself and steps into her magnetic power. Empowering women to believe that everything they need to live happy, fulfilled, aligned lives is already inside of them and walking them home as they flourish and thrive is her soul's purpose.

Margaret believes that mindfulness and inner self work should be relatable, accessible and simplified so even the busiest, most overwhelmed woman can transform her life. Women are often deterred from accessing coaching programs as they can feel too 'woo-woo', too overwhelming or be too expensive. Queen of my Own Universe offers affordable one-to-one personalised coaching with the fundamental premise of connection and belief in self, awareness and accountability, and providing techniques and tools that can create lasting impact in just a few minutes each day.

Having spent over thirty years in corporate workplaces and experiencing firsthand the ever-increasing demands on employees and the devastating impact of workplace stress and burnout, Margaret offers workshops and training for mindfulness activities in the workplace to help employers truly care for employee wellbeing.

An inspiring storyteller, Margaret brings a vulnerability, openness and generosity of spirit to her interactions with everyone, sharing her own lived experiences of trauma, abuse, mental illness, relationship breakdowns, illness and burnout to inspire other women that they can change their own narrative too.

The Mornington Peninsula region in which she lives has a broad demographic, including some lower socioeconomic and underprivileged areas, and Margaret brings free and low-cost mindfulness and life coaching programs to her local community and online globally. She is passionate about connecting women to each other through women's circles and is a volunteer mentor in the Women's Spirit Project.

Website: queenofmyownuniverse.com

STEPPING BACK TO STEP UP

Merendi Leverett

I have found while being a mum, wife/partner and business owner, I have to wear a lot of different hats! Since becoming a single mum to five children – two in primary school, one teen and twin eighteen-year-olds! – I sometimes wonder how I manage it all. I don't have a magic formula, but running my own business for over twenty years as a health clinician and then starting two other businesses in the past eight years has meant I have learnt a lesson or two on how to create calm and balance in the busyness of life. Over the years, I've developed some simple habits to generate calm amongst the chaos that my life has been and continues to be. During my almost eighteen years of being a mum, and now second time around as a single mum, I've had to juggle numerous balls in the air and there are have been many difficult times where I have not only survived, but have thrived.

While I'm no superwoman – although everyone I speak to says I am – I am hoping that by sharing my life experiences and the tips I have learned along the way, something will resonate and help you create some peace and calm in the busyness of your life. I haven't always been a single mum, and to be honest, I am still ashamed to say those words. I feel there is a stigma around it, even if it's not spoken about. The first time I was a single mum, I left my first husband due to financial, emotional, and at the end of the relationship, physical abuse. It felt liberating. I was finally able to rediscover who I was as an individual and run my business how I wanted to, without my ex's critical opinions on how I should be bringing more money home and telling me how I should run my business.

When I met my second partner, I had been a single mum for two and a half years and my business was suffering financially, as I had recently lost major state government funding due to a change in government. Literally overnight, I had to try and replace this funding, which, when you work in health care, is near impossible. I had to make some hard decisions that year which included foreclosing my company, letting go of staff, closing three health clinics and going back to being a sole trader. That experience was a massive hit to my self-esteem. I recognise, looking back now, that was my first experience of burnout, which I wasn't even aware was a thing at the time. Fortunately for me, my new partner was an accountant and tax agent. He was the first accountant I had dealt with who helped me to work out the best plan for moving forward to save my business brand and allow me to continue working for myself.

The next eight months were very difficult. I had disgruntled staff and an ex-landlord threatening legal action. During this time, I experienced the worst hate mail, both online and to my physical mailbox. To this day, I don't know who was responsible, but I could guess … I know I didn't deserve this treatment. I was already at the lowest of lows, and receiving letters in the mail threatening my life and my family, while anonymous people were posting abuse on social media and sending emails, was hard to take. To top it all off, I had to file for personal bankruptcy! That was the biggest blow, and I don't know how I coped, but somehow, I did.

Despite everything that had happened, I couldn't and didn't want to give up. I needed to earn an income to support my children. I refused to rely on my new partner as he was self-employed and still in the early stages of growth with his own business. I couldn't rely on the child support I was receiving from my ex either. So, what did I do? I held my head high, got off the ground, literally dusted myself off and put one foot in front of the other. Friends often say they admire the strength I have to keep getting up and moving forward when adversity hits. It was only recently I discovered the Japanese proverb *nana korobi, ya oki* which means 'fall down seven times, stand up eight'. I realised this describes me well and it has now become my mantra.

My primary school's motto was 'strive for progress', and I have done this my whole life – I strive for more in every aspect of my life. Losing my company was the start of many events that would lead to a further three episodes of burnout that I would experience in an eight-year period. When I had my fourth child to my new partner at the end of 2014, we experienced the unthinkable: my ex-husband refused to return my older children to me. This began what would become a long-term custody battle that continues to this day. The traumatic events that followed have had flow-on affects, both positive and negative. This period of time was the start of me experiencing several more episodes of burnout. As mentioned, it's only with the benefit of time passing that I can even recognise those moments now. Those periods of burnout flew under the radar because I was always in a flight-or-fight response. My beautiful GP, who has been part of this journey with me, told me one day, 'Merendi, think of your patients with chronic pain. They are constantly in pain and will have good and bad days, but they will never actually be rid of their pain. This is like you. You have been dealing with constant stress, you've never had a day, week or month where you haven't had to deal with some sort of stress in your life.' This was so true.

In February 2020, just before COVID-19, my then-partner decided he needed to have his own space and moved out. My ex-husband and his constant emotional abuse had taken its toll on him. At the end of that same year, one of my twins decided he was not going to return to his dad's to live. Despite my ex-husband taking me to court, the judge interviewed my son, which is very rare, and ruled that he and his twin brother were able to choose who they would live with. The twins were three weeks shy of their sixteenth birthday. From that time forward, my son has lived with me full-time and has had minimal contact with his dad, which is his choice not mine. During this same year is when I experienced yet another burnout event. I had been subjected to bullying from my boss. Fortunately, I worked part-time at a university and I was able to take some extended leave. But of course, the stress was still there when I returned to work. The universe, though, had other plans, and that November – the same day my son decided to not return to his father's – I finished up at the university as my contract was not renewed. Little did I know, at the time, this was the push I needed to start my new business, which I had been dreaming of and planning for at least ten years. Until then, the time had just never felt right.

In 2021, my daughter (third child), at the age of thirteen, decided she didn't want to live with her dad either and ran away several times. Again, my ex-husband took me to court, but this time, a different judge ruled she must return to her father. I was able to negotiate through a mediator to have her spend extra time with me from the start of 2022, but she was still not happy with this outcome, as she, too, no longer wished to live with her father. I am now waiting patiently for when she is fifteen or sixteen and able to tell the court herself what her intentions are, but I suspect that once again, my ex will take me to court, as this is his pattern of behaviour. Until this day, I walk on eggshells daily and am constantly on guard watching to see how she is emotionally on any given day. It breaks my heart to see her so angry, frustrated and sad that her dad will not listen to her and grant her wish to live with me full-time.

Today, I continue to slowly recover from the traumas of my past. I have returned to what I know – my first love – exercise physiology and health coaching, to keep the money coming in as I grow my new business and passion of business coaching. I have actively chosen to only work school hours this past eighteen months so I can be present for my five children, especially for my twins who are now in their final year of school. Someone once told me, many years ago, that when your children start school you'll have more time on your hands. Well, I can confirm, in my experience, this is a lie! I have found as my older children have entered high school, they have needed me more, not just emotionally, but also just to be present and available at any given moment. I take comfort in this knowing that they may not always want to talk and share their day, but they want the reassurance that I'm home and available if they need me.

Why am I baring my heart and soul to you? Firstly, I am finding it cathartic to finally be able to write and share my struggles. Secondly, telling you about my own life leads into my advice on how to manage and thrive after burnout. If you only take away one piece of information, I am happy that I was able to help you in some small way.

After I left my husband in 2011, I had lost my identity, so I spent the next twelve months attending meditation retreats and learning self-care in order to recover from the trauma I had endured for such a long time; trauma I had not realised I'd been a victim of. It was over the next eleven years that I trained in many alternative health modalities to help with my own healing, but also so I could help others to heal too.

I am a big believer of ensuring that we, as women, regularly nourish our mind, body and soul and that as mums, wives/partners and daughters, we need to ensure our own buckets are regularly filled. We can't be 100% present and available to our family if we don't take care of ourselves. So, this brings me to my go-to tips that I use regularly to minimise stress, keep me focused and clear in my thoughts, thus ensuring the decisions and actions I make daily, whether it is for business or family, are made from a place of clarity and clear judgement.

1. SET CLEAR BOUNDARIES

It took me a long time to realise I needed to set clear boundaries with not only my clients, but also my family. I was trying to be everything to everyone and this is what contributed to my episodes of burnout. I learnt the hard way that I needed to stand my ground and say no, especially to family. My advice is to have a calendar for family, personal and business to ensure you have all the important events in ALL of them, so you don't forget and end up double-booking yourself. If you work from home, be sure your family knows your work hours and close the door to your home office to minimise interruptions. Do not answer your phone if you are working on a dedicated project or needing uninterrupted time to complete a task. I screen my calls. If it is an unknown number, I let it go to voicemail. If it is one of my children, I will answer as it is often a mini-emergency. If you find you can't *not* answer your phone, then do invest in a VR service to answer and vet your calls. It certainly takes the stress out of having to return calls. If you don't set clear boundaries from the get-go, you are setting yourself up for less productivity and more stress.

2. EXERCISE

Exercise is my go-to the majority of the time, not only because I am an accredited exercise physiologist, but I find exercise is like a moving meditation for me. Whether it is walking my dog or going for a swim, when I exercise, I am able to clear my thoughts, and often, this is when ideas or solutions come to me. The result is that I feel so much better mentally and I find I have a burst of energy, especially if I've had a bad night's sleep or am stressing over something. As a busy mum, how do I fit exercise into my already busy schedule? I have a weekly personal training session booked during school time on my day off. Yes, sometimes I have to miss it due to sick children or other personal commitments like school events, but I don't feel guilty if I have to miss it, as I know I will make it up somewhere else in my week. On the weekends I always try to get my youngest two children and our dog out of the house for a walk to the park, and then on those rare days I do not have children, I may go for a swim. I strongly suggest booking time out in your diary to ensure you dedicate some time to exercise, even if it is only two or three times per week.

3. SELF-CARE

Finally, self-care – and this is the big one! There is a stigma that self-care is negative and is associated with self-indulgence or being selfish. This is so not the case! Self-care is about taking care of yourself so that you can be physically and mentally healthy so you can perform your job, you can care for others and you can do all the things you need to do and want to accomplish. It is about ensuring you can be the best version of yourself and it also helps to reduce stress and anxiety. Self-care is anything that you do for yourself that feels nourishing and happy.

We, especially as women, need to ensure we complete some kind of self-care regularly. According to Google Trends, the number of searches for 'self-care' has more than doubled since 2015, and we know that in today's society anxiety and depression is at an all-time high! So how do I ensure I am partaking in self-care regularly? I make sure that I check in with myself daily and ask:

- *How are you doing?*
- *How are you feeling?*
- *What is your body asking for or needing right now?*

Self-care is not the same for everyone. Everyone has their own go-to self-care practices, and even your own definition might change over time depending on your needs or stressors in your life. Engaging in self-care regularly can help you better prepare for the day and minimise your reaction to stressful events. Self-care activities can be anything that brings you joy or puts a smile on your face.

Here are some examples of self-care activities, and this list is by no means exhaustive:

- Write in a journal and reflect on what you're grateful for each night before you go to sleep.
- Start each day by paying attention to your breath for five minutes.
- Set positive intentions for the day.
- Eat breakfast.
- Put your phone on airplane mode for half an hour each night and release yourself from the flurry of notifications.
- Call a friend just to say hello.
- Take up a relaxing hobby.
- Pick a bedtime and stick to it.
- Exercise daily, even if it is only fifteen to twenty minutes – you will feel good for doing it.
- Read a book in a peaceful spot in the garden.
- Make a cup of tea and drink it quietly with no distractions from technology or other people.
- Take up a new hobby or art and craft activity.

I hope you've found some benefit from reading my chapter and that my journey has inspired you in some way to take action today to improve your current situation and start taking back control of your life. I truly believe we learn best from one another and that no two women's stories are the same. Our personal journeys of overcoming adversity should serve to share our experiences and what worked and didn't for each of us, and that by listening to one another, we learn a new strategy or tool to help us in our journey of life.

MERENDI LEVERETT

Merendi Leverett is a single mother to five children and founder of Merendi Health and Authentic Healthpreneurs. Merendi Health offers exercise physiology, health coaching and injury rehabilitation services, providing personalised service and holistic care to empower their clients to improve and maintain good health, fitness and quality of life. Authentic Healthpreneurs is a bespoke business strategy and coaching business that helps support, guide, nurture and empower female health clinicians to remove their fears, find their inner power and start their own unique and authentic health business.

Merendi has twenty-five years of experience in successfully starting and growing a variety of health clinics in hospitals, universities and private practice. She is a multi-award winner in the Pine Rivers Press Quest Business Innovation Award in 2009 and the AusMumpreneur for Best Service Business and Quest Best Health Care Service in 2010. She has also been nominated three times in the Telstra Business Women's Awards, nominated for the AusMumpreneur Awards in 2012 and 2022, was a nominee for the ESSA Industry Award for Practice of the Year and ESSA Industry Award for Practicum Supervisor of the Year in 2019. Most recently she was a finalist in her local Hills District Chamber of Commerce Inaugural Women in Business Awards. It's fair to say, her work has been widely recognised by her peers!

Merendi loves sharing her knowledge and expertise with other female health clinicians who want to break away from working for someone else to owning their own successful and profitable health clinic. All of this hands-on experience (as she continues to run her own health business twenty years on) allows her to provide her clients with exceptional value and support. She has been a business mentor for over ten years to many inspiring healthpreneurs through USQ, CQU, Exercise and Sport Science Australia (ESSA) and most recently with Business Queensland and Inspiring Rare Birds. She is also honoured to have been asked to be an AusMumpreneur award judge for the past nine years.

Merendi has been writing in the areas of health and wellness for the past fifteen years. She is approached regularly by freelance writers to provide comments, to be an expert panelist/contributor or be interviewed on various health issues and topics current in the media for national newspapers and magazines such as *Herald Sun, Weight Watchers* and most recently *Kiddipedia*.

Merendi has co-authored three books in the past eleven years, including:

- *Amazing Mumpreneurs,* edited by Peace Mitchell and Katy Garner, 2011, Connect2Mums (self-published).
- *Therapeutic Physical Activities,* edited by Li Li and Shuqi Zhang, 2015, Nova Science Publishers Inc. The title of her chapter is 'Therapeutic physical activities for people with low back pain'.
- *Spiritual Discovery Journal,* 2020, Synk Media.

Merendi has also been a podcast host for the past three years. Her most recent series is named *Authentic Healthpreneurs.* She shares the amazing, inspiring and motivating stories of female healthpreneurs and how they came to start their own unique business. Her podcast aims to inspire and educate you on all you need to know about starting, growing and pivoting in business as a health clinician.

FIGHT FOR YOUR HAPPY

NO-ONE ELSE WILL

Dr Monica D Rajasagaram

I was too busy living someone else's dream.

I was busy making sure what I did next didn't upset anyone.

I was busy making sure others understood what I was doing.

Busy was what I knew.

Busy was what I did well.

Busy was easy to keep going with.

Until, it wasn't.

'Why would you do that? Why would you give away all those years of studies you've invested in, to walk away from it now?'

These were the questions I was asked when I decided to dip my toes into something new – the world of coaching – many years ago. It was confusing, frustrating and painful to keep explaining what it was I was trying to do. I had been a medical practitioner for many years. I went through medical school and completed my training years with enthusiasm. My career quickly became my identity. It was the one part of me that felt secure. It seemed like my dream career for a long time, until having my first child, when I felt a stir in my soul for something more.

It was a busy season in my life. It looked and felt great – with a beautiful husband and a young child to raise, there was barely room for much else. My days were full, and each week rolled into another. In the midst of the busyness of life, the longing for something more and the desire for a deeper meaning to life didn't go away. That stir for something more, the questioning of what else was out there for me, came as a shock to me and to those who knew me well. The confusion that followed kept me stuck in a space I didn't anticipate. Having one foot in my medical career and the other in a land of confusion wasn't much fun.

THE STRUGGLE FOR ANSWERS

In the quiet of night, I would lay down after a long day and question if there was more for me. So many questions ran through my head: the *why-this? why-now? what-if?* questions. I was too afraid to ask these questions out loud, simply because I didn't know if it would sound too crazy. Was I losing my mind? Was I being selfish for wanting more than what seemed to be this good life?

With these questions also came the guilt of wanting something different. For all the years my parents had worked to pay off my education overseas, was this even something I should be asking?

As a woman of faith, I also struggled with understanding the *why* behind the confusion I was facing. Why did God bring me all this way through med school, to graduate after so many years, to continue on with my training, only to get to a crossroad in my life and the confusion of *what next?* looming in my head. *Why, God? Why me? Why this confusion?*

I knew deep down what my heart wanted, but my head wouldn't allow for my heart to even explore. Logic told me I would be crazy to throw away years of education and effort and trade it for the unknown.

They do say, 'Be careful what you pray for!' I didn't know it then, but hindsight is a great teacher. Praying a prayer for direction each night in my little walk-in wardrobe seemed pointless at the time. I wasn't seeing a clear path in front of me! I wanted some answers. I wanted someone to show me what I needed to do next to end the frustration I was experiencing in my career. Going to work each day became a 'must do'. I do know that many people feel *they have to go to work* because that's what adults do! There are bills to pay and a life to build. But it wasn't the work I didn't like, in fact, when I sat down to evaluate what it was that I felt was amiss, it definitely wasn't the work. I loved my job and I was honoured to be able to do the work that I did. My patients told me often how they appreciated my work, and I enjoyed working with my colleagues. Yet, I could not put my finger on all the feelings of frustration I had. All I knew, back then, is that something wasn't quite fitting, and something had to change for me to live my life with greater purpose.

As I have now worked with many women who have walked through a similar transition themselves, I can, hand on heart, tell them that to embrace the change that we want for ourselves, we first have to take time to be still and to pause long enough to ask ourselves some difficult questions. Often, we already have the answers, but for many we don't stop long enough to even ask the questions. Why? Because we are simply busy letting life happen *to* us. That was my story, and I see this in the lives of many women I work with.

As I began to open my heart and mind to what was going on around me and for me, I knew that if I was too busy pleasing people and living up to the expectations of others, I was inherently walking away from pleasing God and the calling He had placed on my life. While being a doctor was part of my life's plan, it was not to be the way it ends. I felt in my knowing that God had more for me. But first I had to QUIT BEING BUSY! I had to QUIT IGNORING HIS LEADING. I had to say goodbye to busy.

SAYING GOODBYE TO THE LIFE I ONCE KNEW

Saying goodbye to being busy didn't come easy. There was a gap between asking the questions and saying goodbye to busy, in which I felt confused and unsure of my identity. I journalled for many hours through those months of confusion. I sat in silence listening intently for the still-small voice of God. I shared my heart and my burdens with my husband. Though it felt strange and heavy sharing my confusion and dissatisfaction with life and where I was at, it also felt liberating and freeing at the same time.

Strangely, in that fog of confusion, I was beginning to also see a spark of something new and something fresh that was making me somewhat happy. It was in the far distance, yet it was visible. It felt out of reach, yet reachable at the same time. It felt impossible, yet the hope of possibilities excited me.

What followed these months was the beginning of a great shift. I began to ask many questions of myself – of my wants, desires, visions and goals. I knew this was a journey I was going to possibly be on for a long time, but I had to start exploring my options. I had to dig deep into myself, to get comfortable with the discomfort of change. It's funny how many more opportunities we see when we give ourselves the permission to look! I began to seek help and found myself enjoying conversations that sparked my creative exploration of what was out there. I worked with a coach, I did the work and I leaned into her expertise.

Saying goodbye to busy wasn't something I welcomed easily. Saying goodbye to busy meant I had to start doing things differently. It meant showing up for what brought me joy and saying 'no' to the things that didn't. It meant cultivating what matters in life to me and my loved ones, and putting the things that didn't matter on the back burner. It also meant letting go of expectations I had of myself and what I had hoped my life would look like. Saying goodbye to busy sure was hard, but it taught me lessons I would not have otherwise learnt.

WHAT THE JOURNEY OF TRANSITION REVEALED

I learnt that busy was something I did because I was consumed by the goal I wanted to achieve. I wanted to progress in my medical career *quickly*. I wanted to start a family *quickly*. I wanted to be successful in my life *quickly*. The common theme in my busyness was *quickly!*

Isn't that what busyness does to us? It speeds us up to perform all the things we need to do, to get to where we want to get to, with not much consideration given to the journey in and of itself. The goal becomes the focus point, and we lose the joy of the journey and what it can potentially teach us!

Saying goodbye to busy showed me that I knew how to show up for everyone but myself. I didn't know how much of a toll it took on my body and mind, until it did. In the years of me being busy with work and all that life threw at me, I also suffered five pregnancy losses. Five losses in four years! You would think I should have been clued in to hear what my body was telling me, but being busy masked that for me. With each loss and time to grieve, I was getting more and more exhausted.

Was this the way I wanted to live? Sitting in medical waiting rooms and pathology collection centres on many occasions had me asking myself this very question, *Is this what life should look like for me, Lord?*

As I walked through those years of confusion and the busyness of life, I knew deep within, something had to give. I had to let go of something. I had to let go of the need to please people, the need to live up to the expectations of others and start looking for something better!

HAPPY ... IS IT YOU I'M LOOKING FOR?

My reality check came as I was being prepared for an MRI scan and was asked, 'Are you ready?' After months of suffering from vague symptoms – chest pains, heartburn, backaches and muscle aches – this was the last of investigations. I was hoping for some results, for reasons why I was experiencing these symptoms. Trying to distract myself from the loud bangs of the MRI, I decided to engage in a conversation with myself. Yet again, I asked myself what I wanted from life and my career. But it was in this moment of wondering, *How did I even get here?* that I made a promise to myself, and that was to pay attention to what brought me joy.

In that MRI machine, a life-changing revelation took place. Holding my breath through the confines of the chambers and being in that space with myself confirmed in me a deep desire for change – a life change.

It took me this experience to realise that busy wasn't serving me. Busy was quietly de-energising me, it was bit by bit dimming my light to find joy in the small things of life. And I was determined like never before to find my light again.

PERMISSION TO START AGAIN

We are often our hardest critique. We place high expectations on ourselves, sometimes unknowingly. I had great expectations and a time line that had to work for me and my life. And when that didn't go to plan, I felt out of control. The only control I had was in my career progression, and given that my career was beginning to confuse me, that completely took me off course.

We have to give ourselves the permission to try again and again and again. We have to learn to let go of what could have been and give ourselves the opportunities to create or recreate what could be.

Exploring a new career option wasn't something I had envisioned for myself after so many years. It was scary to even think about. After all, are we not to stay in the one career and make it to the top? Says who!? Is that what we believe for ourselves, or is that an expectation society has placed on us? Neither needs to be true.

What I do know now is this: giving ourselves permission to try again, to recreate again, to explore again allows for us to find ourselves again! As life evolves, so do our desires. And as I mature through life, growing in my faith journey, I have seen this to be truer today. God will never waste any of our life experiences. He uses them all when we partner with Him to explore different opportunities. But first we have to be a willing participant in this process of transition. We have to first take the step in boldness, in obedience to say 'yes' to starting again.

HELLO HAPPY! ARE WE THERE YET?

Can we arrive at happy? Have I arrived at happy?

I see being happy as a by-product of the choices we make in life.

I've had to fight to create a life I now live; I have to be thankful, daily, for the blessings I have and remember to be contented with what I have, rather than be resentful for what I don't.

Does the tendency to be busy fully leave us? I don't think so!

Falling into the trap of being busy is so subtle, it creeps up on us. It starts with a small decision to do or commit to more, followed by the desire to be more. Like a plague, it soon overtakes our entire being, and before long, we are living in the patterns and rush of busy once again.

Saying goodbye to busy should never be a one-off decision. I know I am not there yet, but through the years of lived experience, I know that saying goodbye to busy has to be one of the best things I can continue to do for myself and my loved ones.

I am not there yet, but I am on my way.

You can be too.

Fight for YOUR HAPPY, friend, because no-one else will do it for you!

DR MONICA D RAJASAGARAM

Monica is a certified Maxwell Leadership coach, author, speaker, an accredited Strengths Profile practitioner and a Tiny Habits certified instructor. She is a wife, a mum of two girls and a community builder. Monica is passionate about helping women LEAD and GROW through life, business and faith.

Monica graduated from medicine in 2006 (Monash University, Melbourne), and after working as a medical practitioner for many years, she transitioned into building her coaching and consulting business. Over the years, her business has evolved to serve women in seasons of transition. She is passionate about supporting women in business, or women who are starting one, to learn to lead themselves towards their *own* idea of success. She helps women put in place growth tools and business strategies to create a life and business that is in alignment with their personal values.

Having walked her personal journey of change and starting again in a new career, she understands the challenges women face when trying to step into their dreams and vision, while building a family and home that supports that dream. Apart from coaching and consulting, Monica is also the creator of *The Grow Through Planner* – an award-winning planner for Christian women who want to partner with God daily in their personal life, business and faith.

Building a product-based business in the last few years has been challenging, but Monica has seen this as an opportunity for growth and learning. *The Grow Through Planner* is in its second year of production with an expansion in product range to support women in their unique personal growth journey. *The Grow Through Planner* is stocked across Australia and the US, with increasing numbers of retailers coming onboard.

Monica has been invited to be a keynote speaker at women's events and conferences. She has appeared on radio interviews (89.9 The Light and Vision Radio) to share her expertise in the health, growth and well-being segments. She works with women in a one-to-one capacity and in group programs, as well as continuing to facilitate and host masterminds. She loves building a community of like-minded women who grow together and cheer the progress of each other. Apart from supporting women, she also mentors pre-teen girls through various different programs and platforms.

In her free time, she enjoys reading both fiction and non-fiction, writing and sipping coffee.

Website: drmonicadr.com
Instagram: @monica.d.r & @growthroughplanner

LIVE YOUR LIFE WITH SELF-COMPASSION & RADICAL RESILIENCE

Olivia Ong

On a fine spring day in 2008, my life changed forever. I was walking through the car park of the hospital where I worked when suddenly I was hit by a car at high speed. My body was flung into the air, and as I hovered, as if in slow-motion, a few thoughts ran through my head.

You see, a few years earlier, in my late twenties, I had felt like I'd ticked all the success boxes. I was working as a resident doctor in a reputable hospital, I had my own house and car, and I was happily married with a great network of friends.

Life was great!

But in reality, I wasn't fulfilled. I lacked self-worth.

Being a perfectionist, I used to beat myself up for making the tiniest of mistakes.

I didn't listen to my needs when work got busy. I did my job on autopilot – running around from ward to ward, doing my charts. I even scolded myself for needing to use the bathroom. I actually wished I had a catheter so I wouldn't have to stop working to pee!

I didn't seek help because that would have meant I was weak, incapable – dare I say, not competent. I was isolated, disconnected and helpless.

This was exactly how I felt as I flew through the air after being struck by an old Toyota Camry travelling at 60km per hour. Surely I could have picked a Mercedes!

I landed with an Earth-shattering thud.

I had a spinal cord injury and lost the ability to walk.

As a patient, on the other side of the health care system, the days in the hospital were challenging. This time, I really did have a catheter! I felt like a pin cushion, with drips in my arms and a feeding tube up my nose. I had never felt so vulnerable.

For months after my spinal surgery, I used all my willpower every single day to try and move my legs, but I couldn't.

I felt defeated.

And I felt angry at the driver – an elderly man with severe dementia.

As I lay in the hospital bed, I felt so alone.

Unable to move, I had intense feelings of grief and loss.

Will I ever be able to walk again?

Will I ever be a doctor again? That's my identity, that's all I know …

I'm such a burden to my husband, will he leave me?

Will I ever … have … kids?

My self-worth, which was already low, plummeted to rock bottom. I so badly needed to walk again. Not only because I wanted to be mobile, but because I wanted *my identity* back. Even if it was an identity that lacked self-worth.

One day I heard about Project Walk – a centre for spinal cord injury recovery in San Diego, United States. At first I thought the state-of-the-art technology was what was going to help me, but after three years there, I learned a far more powerful life lesson: self-compassion.

You see, my experience to learn to walk again was the exact opposite of my life as a resident doctor.

Instead of being on autopilot, wishing that I had a catheter so I didn't have to go to the bathroom, I had to be mindful of every step I took.

Instead of being a lone ranger struggling to seek help, I connected with fellow spinal cord injury survivors (my friends on wheels!), bound together by our humanity and our common suffering from spinal cord injury.

Most importantly of all, instead of being a perfectionist beating myself up for every mistake I made, I learned to accept myself for who I was.

Research indicates that self-compassion leads to increased productivity. Self-compassion allows you to remain calm in the face of failure, rejection and criticism. You experience higher wellbeing and are more productive and successful. Self-compassion also leads to reduced stress as it activates our soothing system which leads to greater feelings of wellbeing. Mindfulness, common humanity and self-acceptance – these are the three pillars of self-compassion, and these were the things that gave me self-worth; I realised my self-worth was not attached to my need to walk again and definitely not to the successes I had earlier in life.

I drew inspiration from the ancient Japanese art of kintsugi, which repairs broken ceramics with gold to make them stronger and more beautiful. In the 1400s, Japanese craftsmen started using precious metals, such as gold, to bond together pieces of pottery, thereby drawing attention to, rather than away from, the breaks. This then had the effect of making the break the most important part of the piece itself.

The first time I saw a piece of kintsugi, it was an epiphany. I could relate so well to the concept because it symbolised my whole life. I, too, had been broken, but I was still there, repaired, proud of my experiences and my scars. And stronger than ever.

Kintsugi is a powerful metaphor for self-development. Like the golden fault lines running through the pottery, just as we are broken, we can be repaired – and the manner of that repair, the learning in that growth, becomes a strong and beautiful part of who we are.

After three years doing physical therapy at Project Walk for five hours every day, I finally learned to walk again.

I was over the moon and I went back to my job in Australia happy, enthusiastic and ready to tackle new challenges.

Slowly but surely my self-worth started coming back. I passed my fellowship exams in rehabilitation medicine in 2014, and three years later I passed my fellowship exams in faculty of pain medicine. Far from losing my husband, as I'd feared when I had my accident, we had two beautiful children together.

I had built a beautiful life from something that was traumatic and sad, to become a formidable force in the lives of my family and friends, while earning the respect of my medical colleagues.

Most importantly of all, I learned to respect myself.

But life still had a few more lessons to teach me.

In 2019, I fell facedown with burnout. I was exhausted. I had insomnia and became cynical and sarcastic. To put it bluntly, I was a horrible person to be around.

I was working as a pain specialist and had just finished my pain fellowship exams. I was juggling this full-time position with my disability as well as motherhood, my son being three years old at the time. People would say I was a superwoman. They would say they didn't know how I managed to do it all.

The truth was, I was on the hamster wheel. Working hard, trying to be everything for everyone and putting myself last.

As a result, my energy and wellbeing reached dangerously low levels. The combination of living with a spinal cord injury, motherhood, full-time work and studying intensively for the pain fellowship exams had exhausted me.

I hadn't been okay for years since my injury, and I wasn't looking after myself. Just as I had before my accident, I ignored the warning signs, feeling that burnout was a sign of vulnerability and weakness, so I just kept pushing through.

Not only that, but I was also withdrawing and disconnecting from the people around me. Burnout was slowly wounding my soul. I was barely holding it together, and I secretly wondered how much longer I could go on.

It turns out it would only be a matter of time before I had my face-down moment in 2019, and the full force of burnout took its toll on me.

I had visions of the physician and mother I wanted to be. Deep down, I knew there had to be a way I could build my career while growing my family and become the leader and mother I envisioned, without the burnout.

However, my story of recovery from burnout didn't start with a dramatic declaration of self-compassion and mindfulness. It started from a place of basic human need. To care for my family; to provide for my family. If I wasn't okay, we weren't okay. I needed to be okay. And I wasn't.

From that point, the only possible way was up. I had to recover. I promised myself I would never be in this dark place of burnout again. I realised it was time for me to up the ante on self-compassion, to be 100% responsible for myself and my choices and to stop giving power to others.

Once again, I turned to kintsugi to develop my resilience and strength in recovering from burnout, giving me the tools to overcome adversity and not to be frightened of it.

Kintsugi encourages us to live a full, rich, authentic life, unafraid of the things that might break us. Just as ceramics are fragile, beautiful and strong, so are we. And just as ceramics can break and then be repaired, so, too, can we. Both ceramics and life can break into a thousand pieces, but that's no reason to stop living intensely, working intensely and keeping all our hopes and dreams alive. Adversity is nothing more than a challenge; we just have to work out the right training to overcome it. In 2020, I decided I wanted to rediscover the passion in my work, restore my mental and emotional wellbeing, and reconnect with my family, my inner self and my identity – beyond being a physician. I invested in my recovery by developing my skills in self-compassion and mindfulness to help me feel calm and balanced. I found coaches who guided me through my mindset issues and limiting beliefs. I also discovered creative personal development tools that helped me thrive at home and at work. Together, these taught me how I could take ownership of my thoughts to gain a whole new perspective. Not only was I not willing to live with fatigue and overwhelm, but I knew that if I could change, so could others.

There was one issue I felt especially drawn to: physician burnout and physician suicide. Physician burnout is at an all-time high, with 70% of doctors reporting signs of burnout. On top of that, doctors have the second highest suicide rate of any career.

I have personally seen many of my medical colleagues burnout, as well as experiencing it myself. I realised I could help my medical peers discover these heart-based tools for themselves so they could rediscover their self-worth and lead the heart-centred life they truly deserve. I wanted to help them find their spark of joy and creativity outside of medicine.

I became a life and business coach for physicians so that I could teach the same tools that changed my life. Now, two years on, I have more energy, more time for myself and my family and a renewed sense of purpose.

Once again, I'm drawing on kintsugi to help my fellow doctors who are experiencing burnout. In truth, living intensely and running head-first into your life, without fear, instead of backing away from it, is what ensures we are living lives of true depth and experience. But living this way means opening yourself up to pain. Kintsugi comes in recognising and accepting the role of adversity in our lives. For many people, a moment of crisis – the loss of a job, a divorce, a serious accident – can, with hindsight, be a powerful motive for change and the chance of a new, happier, more deeply lived life.

The pain we feel as we face challenges is one of the most important parts of the human existence. In reality, it is pain that awakens you and makes you feel alive. It will remind you of what is important and how, without darkness, light cannot exist.

It is important that the method of repair in kintsugi is gold – strong but beautiful at the same time, and most importantly, *noticeable*. The precious nature of the gold used to fuse pieces together signifies the strength, confidence and value we can put into repairing our own breaks. For many years, I went through life with parts of my heart that were broken. I watched my medical colleagues and friends move on with their lives while, for many years, I was paralysed and stuck in a wheelchair. I wasn't aware of it then, but I wasn't taking proper care of myself. My experience of learning how to put myself back together made me stronger, tougher and more resilient.

Kintsugi marks our progress. As we grow in strength, we also start to chart our own journey. Just like scars on our bodies (I have a 20cm vertical scar on my upper and lower back from surgery to stabilise my spine), the golden joinery of kintsugi ensures we do not forget what led us to this point and what we have done to move forward. We shouldn't conceal our repairs – they are proof of our strength.

There is still a lot of stigma around doctors seeking help for mental health issues and fear of medicolegal repercussions. There are many doctors suffering silently from mental health issues and burnout. We deserve better. This desire to help doctors through burnout inspired me to set up my speaking and book business, so that I can help physicians around the world to lead the heart-centred life they truly deserve, without the burnout.

We need more heart-centred doctors in medicine. This is my driving force. This is my *why*.

This is me today. I practice, coach and mentor radical resilience. Radical resilience is compassionate and resilient leadership in a modern economy, maintaining high performance and wellbeing and avoiding burnout.

I self-published a book, *The Heart-Centred Doctor,* which talks about self-compassion and physician burnout. Jack Canfield wrote the foreword. After my book launch, I had a lot of PR and publicity, and I'm now a media commentor and professional speaker on burnout.

And the biggest takeaway from this chapter is that I want you all to always remember to live your life with self-compassion and radical resilience.

OLIVIA ONG

Dr Olivia Ong, known as the 'Heart-Centred Doctor', is a pain physician with fifteen years of clinical experience and an expert in resilience and burnout.

After a severe car accident in 2008 left her paraplegic, Dr Ong was told she would never walk or practice medicine again. Dr Ong found out exactly what it's like on the other side of the health care system. She spent years as a patient in hospitals and rehab facilities in Australia and the US in an attempt to regain some of the capabilities that were torn away from her. Little did she know she was going to get a whole lot more than she'd bargained for. After an intensive three-year recovery process, she walked again. Today, she shares her experience with others.

Among other things, coming out the other side of such dark period in her life inspired Dr Ong to start a business to address the unspoken toll that doctors bear when they don't find the support they need. As a high-performance leadership coach and mentor for doctors over the past two years, she runs programs helping doctors transform their lives, moving from burnout to balance.

Being able to speak from her own unique life experiences gives her presentations a deeply authentic feel, and her warm approach has made her a sought-after speaker and online educator. She is the author of *The Heart-Centred Doctor,* which features a foreword from one of her mentors Jack Canfield, co-author of the *Chicken Soup for the Soul* series and *The Success Principles: How to Get from Where You Are to Where You Want to Be.*

Dr Ong has been privately trained by personal development role models such as Jack Canfield; Vishen Lakhiani, founder of Mindvalley; Ajit Nawalkha, founder of Evercoach in Mindvalley; Benjamin Harvey and Cham Tang, founders of Authentic Education; Mike Kim, author of *You Are the Brand;* and Rich Litvin, co-author of *The Prosperous Coach.*

Her vision is for her company, The Heart-Centred Method Institute Pty Ltd, is to be the leading global personal growth and professional development company for physicians and clinicians in health care so that they can be well-rounded, heart-centred health care workers.

Dr Ong has been featured in and written for *Thrive Global, Yahoo Finance, International Business Times Singapore* and *Australian Business Journal.* Dr Ong has regularly appeared in media such as Sky News, Studio 10 and Ticker TV, as well as speaking at industry-leading events including Australasian New Zealand College of Anaesthesia and Faculty of Pain Medicine, where she talks about physician burnout and how mindfulness and self-compassion can transform chronic pain.

Originally from Singapore, Dr Ong now resides in Melbourne, Australia, with her husband and two young children. Her forthcoming book, *Radical Resilience,* is due to be released in early 2024.

Website: drolivialeeong.com

ONE MINUTE CAN CHANGE YOUR LIFE

Peace Mitchell

'Why on Earth are you doing one minute of yoga?' she laughed when I told her about what I'd planned.

And it was funny. Even I thought it was funny. But if my plan worked, perhaps it wouldn't be so funny after all. Maybe it would be the one thing that could save me.

This was January, but I'm getting ahead of myself. If we're going to start, we need to start with November. Or as it came to be known, 'Donevember'. It had been a busy but productive year; new projects had proved to be profitable, but others had been lots of work with little financial return due to circumstances beyond our control. Events had to be rescheduled and mass refunds paid, which added stress to our small business. Somehow, everything had been pushed to November in a rush to get the year wrapped up before Christmas. We had around eight different projects that we'd been working on for months, culminating in these four short weeks.

These included:

- A book launch of an anthology with thirty-six authors travelling across the state to host a three-day, in-person conference for 120 people, followed by an awards gala dinner for two hundred people.

- A five-day online festival featuring forty presenters.
- An international virtual pitch night with twelve tech founders.
- Two other pitch nights for our graduating class of twenty-five business students, with each pitch night requiring separate, special guest investor panels, volunteer commitments and more.

It was exhausting mentally, physically and emotionally. Dealing with so many different people, each requiring different things and expecting us to be across every detail of every project, we'd taken on too much and the stress was a lot to cope with.

But even the hardest of times end, and finally, it was done. We really needed a break, but instead of a break, we were looking forward to 'Funcember', a time when we would hire a lake house, bring both of our families and create special memories with our combined seven children plus their partners. It should have been restful and relaxing, but we'd spent so long dreaming about a magical family Christmas by the lake with all the cousins that we ended up planning elaborate meals and wild Christmas-themed activities, requiring even more work from us.

By the time we got to January, I was too tired to even make a vision board, something I normally use to plan for the year. I knew something had to change. I couldn't keep running on empty and doing everything for everyone else with nothing left for myself.

But what could I change and how would adding more create less?

Around the same time, I'd read a book on habits. It talked about the Olympians who work on investing hours of time and research to improve their time, efficiency or speed by just 1%. I'm talking milliseconds. In some sports, like swimming, they investigate every miniscule detail, like whether the type or thickness of fabric of the swimwear can make a difference to the speed. I was fascinated by the idea of using small increments and improvements to get different results. The book also explained that when people had been in bad accidents and had to learn to walk again, they always started with very short sessions and simple exercises on the first day, and then very gradually worked towards longer sessions each day. I found this so inspiring. What was possible for me if I started small with something and kept working at it little by little every day? Could I achieve something incredible too?

I knew I had time for this. I wake up early every day and have a solid two hours to myself. Often, that time is caught up in bad habits like endlessly scrolling social media or getting my laptop out and filling that two hours with answering emails and working, or even cleaning the house. I'd made a conscious decision long ago to dedicate this precious time to self-care instead, but somehow that wasn't happening – I just wasn't sure how to structure the time. It seems ridiculous, but unless I had an actual plan for self-care, this time would just keep getting swallowed up by work, social media and everything else.

I was curious about yoga. I'd heard people rave about how life-changing it was, and I'd found a YouTube yoga teacher I liked, Adriene from Yoga with Adriene. She ran thirty-day online yoga programs you could watch anytime and follow each day. I'd joined in a couple of times and always enjoyed it. I'd felt better afterwards, but after a little while I'd forget about it, or get bored with doing a full thirty-minute class. Sometimes I'd sleep in and run out of time. I struggled to maintain consistency and found I was beating myself up for not doing a full class or missing a few days, then quitting altogether after missing a couple of days in a row.

I wondered if I could try again but this time do it differently. It was clear I needed to start small and work up slowly, rather than expecting myself to just jump in to a thirty-minute class every day. From the start, I wanted to create a manageable and lasting habit. I realised I needed to be kinder to myself and not beat myself up for all the times I would inevitably fail. And by fail, I mean sleep in, feel unwell, run late, not feel like it, have something urgent come up, be travelling or away from home, have to cut the time shorter etc. etc.

I was ready to do things differently and create a lasting habit that was so easy I could stick to it.

But even more importantly, I was determined to change my life and commit to investing in myself and my own wellness and wellbeing.

I remember waking up on that first day, excited but also nervous. Would it work? Was this ridiculous? Would I be able to commit to this? Would I sleep in? Would I forget and then quit again? Would all the reasons it hadn't worked in the past happen again this time? Would this be another way for me to let myself down?

I didn't want anything to get in the way of me and that one minute of yoga. I wasn't going to add any extra steps that would be an excuse like changing out of pyjamas into yoga gear or setting up my yoga mat every day. I just wanted to wake up and do yoga, then get on with my day.

It was ridiculous doing one minute of yoga. Of course I can do a thirty-minute session; I've been to ninety-minute classes before. But I had made a plan and I knew it was important to make it easy for the first few days. They say that if you can keep a daily habit going consistently for eight days, you're more likely to keep that habit going for long enough for it to become a long-term habit.

On day two I did two minutes, on day three I did three minutes. I was so proud of myself by day seven because when I added up the number of minutes each day, I'd completed twenty-eight minutes in total over the week – and that's not 'nothing'.

On day eight, however, I woke up with a really bad headache. Was this the end for my thirty days of yoga? In the past, it definitely would have been, especially if I'd pressured myself into the impossible perfection of maintaining daily thirty-minute classes.

But not this time. This time, I'd promised to be kind to myself.

So on day eight, I poured myself a big glass of water and found a slow and relaxing YouTube class for 'yoga for illness' and just did the first eight minutes of it. Yoga is actually known for its therapeutic and healing benefits, but not all classes are right for when you have a headache and some are way too intense. YouTube is an incredible resource library for discovering exactly what you need when you need it.

On day fifteen, we went away for the weekend. I'd had a big night and woke up too late to fit in yoga. Instead of beating myself up for missing it, I forgave myself and recommitted to starting again the next day. This was a big step, and I believe, a really important part of the process for me.

My plan was to increase my daily yoga by one minute a day all the way up to day thirty where I did thirty minutes. Once I got to day thirty, I promised myself I could reset and start again with a new challenge. I'd accidentally found a way to make creating a habit fun and flexible, and I realised that this was much more aligned with my values of freedom, fun and creativity than the usual rigid practice I'd tried in the past.

There aren't any thirty-day yoga programs that follow this process of one minute a day then two minutes a day that I know of, so I used YouTube and searched by the number of minutes to find new yoga classes every day. By doing this over the thirty days, I got to try out lots of different types of yoga and lots of different yoga instructors.

When I finally got to day thirty, I was so excited. I was so proud of myself for sticking to the promise that I'd made to myself. I didn't want it to end, but I'd now found my flow and my morning yoga had become my daily commitment to myself. Reaching thirty days was a milestone that I'm still proud of now. I'd never done this before in my life, and now that I knew it was possible, I wondered what else would be possible for me.

After that first thirty days, I then began one of the thirty-day yoga programs I had tried in the past. Would this work, or would it be a failure again? Would it be too boring to do the same thing every day? I really didn't know. But the beauty of habits is that once you've established them, you've seen results and you're committed to them, it's much easier to keep them going.

This time around I recommitted to giving myself permission to be kind to myself, and it has really worked so much better. If I'm having a slow day (like when I'm unwell or haven't had enough sleep or need to get going early), I'll still do yoga but I'll choose a gentle practice or do a shorter session. YouTube is incredible. There's so much variety to choose from and yoga for just about everything you can think of, including yoga for when you're on a plane, yoga for when you're tired or yoga for inspiration.

After one hundred days it had become my non-negotiable. Every day started with yoga, and it's something I would look forward to, not an overwhelming chore I had to get through. I found that you don't need much equipment or space, which meant when we were away for the weekend, I could easily fit in a short session, and unlike walking or jogging, it doesn't matter if it's raining outside.

I've definitely got stronger, fitter and more toned too, but I think the main benefit for me is the self-care and committing to myself and my wellbeing, so that even on busy days, I know that I've given myself a window of time to slow down, tune in to my thoughts and reflect before I start my day.

I've learnt that it's not about how perfect you balance in tree pose or how long you can plank for, what's important is showing up for yourself on the mat every day. Putting yourself first even though there are so many other things you could be doing, like folding washing or putting away dishes or answering emails or making the school lunches. All of those things will still be there when you're done.

I've also learnt new things about myself. That I can achieve big things if I start small. That I will fail sometimes, and that it's important to be kind to myself and try again the next day. That I can find new ways to try things that didn't work. That I can find creative ways to make hard things be fun and easy. And perhaps, most importantly, that I can make promises to myself and keep them.

One minute of yoga changed my life. What could one minute change for you?

PEACE MITCHELL

Peace Mitchell is the CEO and co-founder of The Women's Business School, AusMumpreneur and Women Changing the World Press. She is the Australian ambassador of Women in Tech and the chair of global non-profit Tererai Trent International. Peace is also an international keynote speaker, TEDx speaker, bestselling author of *Back Yourself, Courage and Confidence* and *The Women Changing the World,* host of *The Best & Brightest* podcast and *Forbes* business expert.

Peace is passionate about supporting women to reach their full potential. She has helped thousands of women achieve their dream of running a successful and profitable business and believes that investing in women is the best way to change the world. Peace received the Thought Leadership Award at the Stevie Awards in 2022, Diversity in Tech Mentorship Award in 2021 and the PauseFest SuperConnector Award in 2020.

Peace Mitchell co-founded AusMumpreneur in 2009 creating Australia's number-one community for mums in business and co-founded The Women's Business School in 2016 to provide entrepreneurial education for women globally. Together with her business partner, Katy

Garner, she has brought together a community of over 150,000 women in business from around the world.

Today, her commitment is stronger than ever to invest in the power of women to change the world.

THE POWER OF YOUR VISION

Tina Ranoso Bangel

If you're reading this book you are most likely a person filled with dreams and aspirations.

Let's rewind to 2019 – it was going to be my year! I had big plans and big dreams. I love the new year. It means new beginnings and a fresh start!

But then April came along, and I found myself unusually fatigued. I would climb the stairs and my heart would palpitate. I needed daily afternoon naps, and by 3pm my energy was depleted. Unusually, I had a craving for ice and eucalyptus lollies.

I was also gaining weight and couldn't get rid of my excess tummy.

Being constantly bloated, I became weak and depressed. I visited my doctor, and that week, had an ultrasound and CT scan. They couldn't find my left ovary; my uterus was so big it had grown up to my rib cage.

A uterus should be the size of a pear. In the CT scan, they found a 19cm growth. As suspected, I was depleted in iron and had fibroids. Fibroids are non-cancerous growths in or around the uterus. Many women get them, and in some cases, they can be life-threatening. I was told it would be best to have a full hysterectomy; they needed to operate.

The first thing that came to mind was my schedule. Running a business and having over forty students to shuffle is a singing teacher's nightmare. I also had to think of my upcoming gigs. I had a once-in-a-lifetime opportunity to sing with award-winning international stars David Pomeranz and Melissa Manchester at the Sydney State Theatre. It was one of my dream venues, and after all the years of working up to this level, I just couldn't bear to miss the opportunity. I was also scheduled to be in *Marie Claire* magazine – another opportunity I'd been working towards for years. I couldn't reschedule that!

So, the next available operation date was September. My thinking was, *What's another few months – I've carried this thing for years!* September came, and I looked like I was about to give birth. My gynaecologist asked me to get an MRI because she thought it had grown too fast. Luckily, that came back clear of cancer. I fell sick with bronchitis the week of the operation. I prepped for the operation only to be sent home. They wouldn't operate as I had a chance of getting pneumonia with the procedure. I rescheduled again – to November. November came, and I grew 10kg heavier, the fibroid now 30cm in diameter; the biggest the surgical team had ever operated on.

Thank God the operation was successful. I am now fully recovered and my healing is ongoing.

I am now more aware of taking care of my body, mind and spirit. This was the universe or God's way of shouting, *Slow down and pay attention!* I had a choice: hide in a hole and stay depressed, stuck and in blame mode, or create from a loving space. A space of gratitude. A space where I found peace and simplicity.

I simplified everything. I declined gigs, invitations to events and gatherings. While on my hospital bed and at home recovering, I was constantly given signs and treasures. I started my gratitude journal.

Here are just some of the things I listed that brought me joy:

- The countless times my son's lola and lolo (grandmother and grandfather in the Filipino language – Taglog) would show up unexpectedly at our doorstep with a pot full of chicken arroz caldo (a type of chicken rice porridge) – my comfort food and the Filipino version of soul food. I took myself down memory lane where Lola, the kids and I would sit down at the table to make hundreds of lumpia Shanghai (deep-fried spring rolls) for the family gatherings. Wrapping the lumpia was meditative and it was a chance to catch up with the latest news, while visiting Lola's backyard where she propagated her succulents, and seeing them flower or picking her home-grown fruits and vegetables.

- I got back to listening to old classics; songs that gave me comfort and fed my soul. I was also grateful for my husband, my son and my dog Gloria, who became my therapy dog. Food, family and music was the common thread. It inspired me to create a children's storybook called *My Lola*. This book represents joy, simplicity and love all tied in with the Filipino culture and music. My hope is to inspire our kids to embrace our beautiful Filipino culture and food through our love of singing, music and dance! My vision is to see the joy on kids' and parents' faces as we sing and dance during our 'My Lola music and movement classes' and then share some lumpia and calamansi juice after class.

I was lucky I found my way of healing. Yours could look different. There is no right or wrong. So let me ask you … are you paying attention? Is it time to put yourself first? Or are you caught up in the wheel of getting things done, robotically ticking off the boxes on your to-do list? Is it time to start that passion project? It is time you follow your dream? What brings you joy?

I'd like to share with you the process I take my coaching clients through during my workshops and courses. I know this works. I've seen students sing on the Sydney Opera House stage with international Broadway stars and the Sydney Symphony Orchestra after just writing down this exact dream six months before. I've seen students have dreams of songwriting, and just months later, they made the national news about their inspirational song. Let's reclaim your true desires. Let's endeavour to find your joy and what you want with no fear, shame or inhibition. Let's connect with your real passion.

How do I do that? you might ask. Well, the answer is to honour your preferences, no matter how big or small. Don't think of your desires as petty. They are your own desires. Inside every one of us is a tiny seed of the 'you' that you were meant to become. Unfortunately, you may have buried this seed in response to your parents, teachers, coaches and other role models as you were growing up. You started out as a baby knowing exactly what you wanted. You would cry if you were hungry or needed to get changed or cuddled. As you got older, you crawled around and discovered your surroundings. You knew exactly where you wanted to go and headed towards it with no fear or inhibitions. Then somewhere along the way someone said, 'Don't touch that!' and, 'Stop crying, don't be a baby!' and, 'You don't really feel that way.'

Then, as you got older, you heard … 'Money doesn't grow on trees,' and, 'You can't have everything you want!' The lesson here is: don't live someone else's dreams. We lost touch with the needs of our bodies and the desires of our hearts, and somehow, we got stuck trying to figure out what other people wanted us to do. We learnt how to act and how to get their approval. As a result we now do a lot of things we don't want to do, just to please a lot of other people.

We get a real job instead of pursuing our dream career in the arts.

We go to university instead of taking a year off to backpack through Europe.

In the name of being sensible, we end up becoming numb to our own desires.

Stop settling for less than you want. To reclaim your power and find your joy, you will have to get rid of these sentences:

- I don't know.
- I don't care.
- It doesn't matter to me.

When you are confronted with choices – no matter how small or insignificant – act as if you have a choice. Ask yourself, *If I did know, what would it be? If I did care, which would I prefer? If it did matter, what would I rather do?* Not being clear about what you want and making other people's needs and desires more important than your own is simply a habit. The goal of my chapter is to get you from where you are to where you want to be. To accomplish this you have to know where you are now and where you want to get to. Your vision is a detailed description of where you want to be. It describes in detail what your destination looks and feels like.

To create a balanced and successful life that brings you joy, your vision needs to include the following seven areas:

- Work and career.
- Finances.
- Recreation and free time.
- Health and fitness.
- Relationships.
- Personal goals.
- Contribution to the larger community.

At this stage of your journey, it's not necessary to know how you will get there but it is important you get clear on the 'what'. Trust the how will show up. Decide on where you want to go by clarifying your vision. Just like a GPS in a car, lock in your destination through goal setting, affirmations and visualisation, and then start moving in that direction.

Stay focused, and the exact steps will keep appearing along the way. When you visualise your goals as already complete each and every day, it creates structural conflict in your subconscious mind between what you are visualising and what you currently have. Your subconscious mind works to resolve that conflict by turning your current reality into the new.

This causes three things to happen:

1. It programs your brain's reticular activating system (RAS) to start letting into your awareness information to achieve your goals. (The RAS is a bundle of nerves that sit in your brainstem. Its job is to regulate behavioural arousal, consciousness and motivation.)

2. It activates your subconscious mind to create solutions for getting the goals you want. Get ready to find ideas popping into your head in the shower, while driving or on your long walk.

3. It creates new levels of motivation. You'll find yourself feeling confident to speak out at meetings, asking for what you want and taking more risks.

The RAS works wonders. It will seek out and capture all the information necessary to bring what you visualise into reality. Be aware that if you feed it negative, fearful and anxious pictures, it will work to achieve those too. One of the easiest ways to stop settling, reclaim your lifelong dreams and find joy is to make a list of thirty things you want to do, thirty things you want to have and thirty things you want to be before you die.

THE POWER OF A VISION BOARD

As I write this I'm watching and hearing the rain fall. We look at rain and the grey clouds as dreary and gloomy, but without rain there would be no rainbows. What if we look at it as a clean slate, a time to renew and start over? One thing that has helped me with making a new start is listening to what I really want. Be still.

I'm going to share with you a process that I love to do – it's creative, it's exciting, but most of all, it takes you back to yourself, to what you really truly want. When creating a vision board, remember it's not set in stone, you can add or delete. You are allowed to change your mind or leave it to the side until it's time for it.

Let's create a vision board of the things we want to invite into our lives. What does success and joy look like to you?

What is a vision board?

A vision board is a visual representation of your wants and desires. What you want to do, what you want to be and what you want to have.

What you will need:

- A3 paper.
- Pen.
- Magazines.
- Photos.
- Words.

What to include:

- Statements.
- Words that light you up.
- Words that make you feel abundant.
- Poems.
- Photos that make you feel alive and speak to your soul.

Think about what you would like to attract into your life and balance it with mindfulness and health in mind.

If you love to surround yourself with people, add people and family into the board. Are you filling your life up with items and things that bring you joy? Are you a plant lady? Does collecting green plants make you smile? Do you need to reawaken your love for drawing? What about cooking? Which childhood recipe brought you excitement? Be creative. Think about the seven areas in your life and what will bring you absolute joy. Once you have finished gluing the pictures and words and designed your vision board, close your eyes and think about what you have created on your board. Close your eyes and breathe in the feeling you get from what you have created. Feel the feelings that your board has given you. Do you feel the abundance, do you feel the joy, do you feel the love, do you feel healthy? Do you feel content?

List the feelings you get from your vision board
Write down which item on your vision board will most light you up and you can start moving towards it becoming a reality.

Don't leave here without writing your own and singing your own song.

When you go for your dreams, while remembering to look after your health and wellbeing, it's amazing how it will inspire people around you to go for their dreams too.

For maximum impact, be sure to share your vision
Don't let anyone talk you out of your vision. There will be people who will tell you it can't be done. Share it with a good friend, someone you trust, someone that is positive and supportive. When you share your vision, you'll find some people will want to help you make it happen. You may also find that every time you share your vision, it becomes clearer and feels more attainable and real. Most importantly, you will strengthen your own subconscious belief that you can achieve it.

I hope my chapter has added to the spark and you have extra kindling to continue to light your joy. Don't forget to pass the flame on by sharing what you've learnt within the pages of this book. Keep the joy alive and may you continue to be blessed.

TINA RANOSO BANGEL

Tina Ranoso Bangel is a vocal coach and professional singer who has inspired thousands of students to use singing as a form of personal development. A graduate from the Australian Institute of Music and a certified neurolinguistic programming master practitioner, Tina is the founder of the One Voice School of Singing.

She has developed and worked with singers who have been a part of *The Voice, The X Factor* and *Australia's Got Talent*. Her students have performed at Disneyland, Universal Studios, Radio City and in major musicals such as *The Lion King* and *The Sound of Music*.

Tina and her students are often asked to provide backing vocals or support international celebrities such as Tony Award-winning Broadway star, Lea Salonga. She was a finalist of the international What's on 4 Kids Awards for Most Outstanding Activity Leader (five to twelve years). She has also held successful charity concerts and crowdfunding campaigns for Red Kite and KidsXpress. In 2021, she was awarded AusMumprenuer people's choice diversity and inclusion award.

During Harmony Week 2022, she performed for the unveiling of the

Australian National Monument to Migration where she sung songs loved by Filipinos around the world.

She is the author of *My Lola* (which translates as *My Grandmother* in Tagalog), a children's book which celebrates Tina's Filipino heritage including food, family traditions and music. She currently conducts Little Voices music and movement experiences in child care centres.

Tina is the host of the *One Voice Can Change the World* podcast. She has been featured in *Marie Claire*, *The Huffington Post*, *Inspired Coach*, *SBS* and *The Daily Telegraph*. She lives in Sydney with her husband, son and their mini foxie.

Tina is currently training to be a certified trainer on Jack Canfield's *The Success Principles*.

MANIFEST YOUR HAPPY

Zhanna Gee

I am a big believer in manifesting. Everything I have today that I hold dear to my heart is something I have attracted into my life. My beautiful family, my husband, our health, our home, my brands, our dogs, our financial freedom and all the little extra joys, like my dream car and closet. Coming from somebody who has quite literally spoken my dream life into existence, trust me when I say society is moving at the fastest pace in the history of mankind … You do not have to fear dreaming big in an age where anything is possible.

I think there is a huge misconception when people who aren't familiar with the term 'manifesting' hear about it. Manifesting does not, by default, have to have a spiritual connotation. There is a real science behind it and studies have been emerging and solidifying what we have felt is true for years. Take a moment to consider that anything and everything you know in our world is made up of energy.

We have our senses in which we can see, touch, hear, smell and taste – but what about the energy that exists outside of our senses? Do you believe that it simply does not exist because the limits of our human body cannot process it? Manifesting a reality you dream of becomes a possibility when you tap into the unknown – at least, this is what I have learnt in my experience. And so far, I'm pretty pleased with how it's working for me!

I have been practicing manifestation for the last fifteen years (consciously) in a variety of different ways – visualisation being the most prominent.

After freshly breaking away from a violent and abusive relationship ten years ago, I sat in my small apartment dreaming of a happier life. I was a single mum who worked a nine-to-five job, making just enough money to pay my bills and get by. Not only was life financially grim, but I felt I was missing out on quality time with my daughter. She was growing so quickly, becoming her own person, and my biggest stressor was how I would financially sustain our lives.

After longing and longing for improvement in any way, I decided to take what I knew about manifesting seriously. Why? Because I had reached a point where I realised that nobody was going to come and save me. Within just one year, I had manifested my dream partner, a new successful career path, financial stability and a *balanced* lifestyle, in which I *could* go to my daughter's school events and be there to watch her grow.

So, how did I do this? How did I go from constantly *wanting* more to constantly *receiving* more? With a piece of paper and a glass of water. That's the no-bullshit truth of it.

Knowing that I had to create a new frequency within myself to attract what I was trying to attain, I began to visualise my future every single day. I began to feel into what I wanted, every single day.

On a piece of paper, I wrote down some short intentions – all in the present tense.

I have a successful brand.
I am financially independent.
I have time to spend with my daughter.

I am in a loving, respectful relationship.
My daughter and my partner have become best friends.
My partner loves my daughter like his own.
I live in my own home with my family.

These were some of the things I wrote down on my piece of paper that I placed on my bedside table, underneath a glass of water. Every morning, whilst drinking my glass of water, I would read all the intentions on the list.

Now despite this sounding like the simplest thing in the world, keep in mind that you can read and say positive affirmations until you're blue in the face, but if you do not *feel* these intentions, you cannot attract your dreams from the unknown.

Whilst reading this list, I would take a moment to ask myself, *How does this feel?* How does it *feel* to own a successful brand? How does it *feel* to be financially independent? What does it look like to live these intentions? I would visualise and materialise, in every way, what it would be like to live like the woman I wanted to be.

Then, after drinking my glass of water and taking the time to truly feel into the existence I was trying to create, I would fill up my glass of water ready to repeat my manifestation process that evening.

Like everything in existence, water, too, is made up of energy, and in recent years science has begun to uncover its ability to take on the frequency of words, sounds and intentions. Whether that's something you give weight to or not, I would place my piece of paper under my water to 'charge' it with my intentions. If one of my intentions had been achieved, or if I had wanted to make a change to my list, I always rewrote the list rather than crossing things out. Never did I want to strike my intentions away or reject the possibility of their existence, I would simply redirect my attention to new or altered possibilities.

As I mentioned earlier, within the first year of doing this I had met my now-husband, who instantly connected with my daughter. Their friendship and bond was even more special than I had hoped it would be. My first brand began to take off, and after years of trying to keep my head above water, I finally felt like I was swimming. I was no longer just surviving, I was thriving.

Ten years on, I am happily married, now with *two* beautiful daughters. I live in my own home with my husband and youngest, our two dogs and a cat. The brand that got me off my feet and began as a side-hustle is now a million-dollar business employing countless other women. I have won multiple awards for the work I've done in my field and I work closely with women's charities. I have time to spend with my children, and most of all, I am happy.

Recently, I found one of the first little notes of intentions I had ever written to myself. All there was to do was smile and thank the universe. I had attracted everything I had once only dreamed of.

Nowadays, making use of manifestation and visualisation hasn't stopped for me. In fact, it's safe to say I have taken it up a notch or two since beginning with a glass of water … Visualising my future and truly *feeling* into it has shown me what can happen when the creativity of daydreaming meets the clarity of goal setting.

Mentally rehearsing *anything* – whether it be good or bad – will start to create bridges and connections in the brain. These thoughts will become *who you are* after a matter of time.

So with that in mind, it is vital to take time out of your day to purposefully create good thoughts. even if it's as quick of a moment as having a glass of water. Visualisation holds far more gravity in the formation of our goals than we, in society, give it credit for. It can create excitement, instil fear and cultivate joy. And yet, somehow, transforming positive mental imagery into a physical form is still not common practice.

After years of fine-tuning how to manifest my dreams, I can say with confidence that visualisation has changed my life. To some, this may make me crazy, but it is what works for me, time and time again. Now, I definitely take the extra step beyond my initial 'list and water' routine, so take a moment to find what method works best for you.

THE SECRETS TO SUCCESSFUL VISUALISATION

1. Clarity

Clarity is vital. Before you begin to visualise your goals, are you clear on what you want to achieve? Are your goals truly yours? Are you dreaming for an outcome that comes from within and *not* from external pressure? Don't waste time chasing dreams for somebody else. Get clear on who you are, what you hold dear and what you want to achieve.

2. Solitude

Having time alone matters. To achieve clarity, you need to know who *you* are without your 'buffers'. Smartphones, television, music, radio, even friends and family – these things create a buffer between you and your soul. When was the last time you were alone in silence with nothing but your own thoughts? Practice solitude to gain clarity.

3. Write it down

If you couldn't tell from the rest of the chapter, I love a written note or two. Write down on a piece of paper all that you wish to bring into your reality, in the present tense.

4. Details

Once you have established what you really want, bring into focus the details. Use your senses to draw attention to the limitless possibilities. The more detail the better, for it will help you to truly feel into your manifestations.

5. Vision board

I'm serious! Once you know what you want, once you can feel into how you want to feel, create a vision board that creates cues for these emotions to come up throughout the day. Vision boards are typically a collection of images that have been carefully curated to reflect a person's goals, dreams and aspirations. Often, the power of creating a physical replica of your mind's eye is overlooked. Turning your thoughts into something physical instantly takes them a step further than 'just' being a dream. Did you know most of our cognition follows our visual perception? When we focus on something we want that we can also see outside of our bodies, our brains naturally want to take action to manifest that desire into a reality. For instance, when you drive by a beautiful home, meet someone with an inspiring career or see a family enjoying themselves happily, thoughts of desire and drive can often be triggered. You may feel motivated, inspired or hopeful that you, too, may achieve this outcome someday … And you can! This feeling of desire is a sure sign that what you're seeing is part of the dream life you want to create, and you'll naturally receive a dopamine hit to take inspired action towards making those dreams a reality! Therefore, having a visual representation, like a vision board, of all that you wish to achieve is such a powerful tool. Every time you view it, you'll receive sparks of inspiration to take more action towards your dream reality. So go on, get some magazines, scissors, pens and start putting your dreams on a piece of paper.

6. Create space

When taking the time to visualise your goals, especially when creating a vision board, make sure you are in a safe space. Not just safe physically, but emotionally. Put yourself into a space where your creativity feels safe to come out. Whether this be in your home or in nature, find somewhere that feels aligned with the energy that *you* want to cultivate. Remember not to take on external opinions and creations that don't serve *you*.

7. Activate

Emotions carry so much energy and are the charge to our intentions. Once you have established what you want, really bring focus into how it *feels* to be the person you want to be. Use all of your senses and more. Truly feel into the existence that you are going to attain, and use your vision board to help you to feel these elevated emotions.

8. Gratitude

Once feeling the emotions of your goals, feel into *gratitude*. Even if it is your first day ever trying to manifest, pause to truly embody what it would be like to already have achieved your dreams. Give thanks to *yourself* for trusting that you can achieve your dream life.

These are my personal tools that I live by to create the life I want. If you can take away anything from me, let it be this: *You are the creator of your life.* It is completely and entirely yours. Nobody can feel or experience the world in the way that you do. You can have coaches, mentors, supporters and loved ones who can advise you and guide you through *their* lens of life, but only you have the capacity to experience this life as you. With this in mind, allow yourself the chance to see how far you can take it. See what *you* are capable of creating and cultivate your own joy and your own happiness.

You now have all my actionable steps and tangible tools to help you be who you want and who *you deserve.* In the worst-case scenario, take a moment out of your day to drink a glass of water whilst thinking some nice thoughts. But in the best case … well – I'll leave that part up to you.

ZHANNA GEE

Immigrating from Latvia over twenty years ago, with English as her third language, Zhanna Gee is a loving wife, mother of two daughters, heartfelt entrepreneur, compassionate leader, author and women's advocate. She builds ecommerce companies that bring millions of dollars to the economy, smashes records in her industry, has insatiable appetite for knowledge and absolutely adores the people she works with. She is fascinated with human design that provides her with valuable tools for self-discovery, correct decision-making and peak performance.

Zhanna is a multi-award-winning entrepreneur, and her brand, Slim By Nature (SBN), has become a leader in the health and wellness industry. SBN is a multi-award-winning brand that has spent the last ten years helping tens of thousands of people around the world transform their health and better their livelihoods. Partnering with industry-leading experts in Australia and armed with full-time professionals, Zhanna and her team have developed a range of award-winning, Australian-made supplements, detox/weight-loss programs, educational courses and wellness products that are backed by science and produce life-changing results.

Breaking away from a once violent and abusive past, today, Zhanna is a passionate women's advocate who challenges adversities by inspiring other women to dream big. With her exciting new brand, Delicious Dreams, due to launch in August 2022, Zhanna is thrilled to bring not only a completely unique brand to the Australian economy but show today's society how to create the life you desire through the power of manifestation.

THIS BOOK CHANGES LIVES

Proceeds from the sale of *Goodbye Busy, Hello Happy* go to providing marginalised women in business with scholarships to enable them to receive support, mentoring and education through The Women's Business School.

Aligning with the United Nations SDG goals for gender equality, The Women's Business School scholarships are awarded to women in remote and rural areas, First Nations women, migrant women, survivors of domestic violence, women with disability and chronic illness and those facing financial hardship.

We believe that investing in women is the most powerful way to change the world and these scholarships provide opportunities for deserving women to participate in an incubator program for early stage startups and businesses and an accelerator program for high potential and experienced entrepreneurs ready to scale their companies and expand globally.

You can read more about the work of The Women's Business School Scholarship Program and how they're changing the world here:

thewomensbusinessschool.com/scholarship

ABOUT PEACE & KATY AND SPEAKING OPPORTUNITIES

Peace and Katy are the dynamic duo behind AusMumpreneur, Australia's #1 community for mums in business, The Women's Business School providing dedicated education for aspiring and established female founders, Women Changing the World Press, amplifying the voices of thought leaders, female founders and women changing the world and Women changing the World Investments, providing opportunities for capital for female founders.

Peace Mitchell is a TEDx speaker, international keynote speaker, retreat facilitator and workshop presenter.

If you want your audience to be captivated by a heart-centred, warm and engaging thought leader and speaker then look no further.

With experience delivering keynote presentations on connection, business success, magic and productivity, there's nothing Peace loves more than engaging with your delegates to make your event a huge success.

If you've got an online or in person event coming up and want to create a magical, warm and engaging atmosphere, please get in touch.

peace@womensbusinesscollective.com
+61 431 615 107

ABOUT THE WOMEN'S BUSINESS SCHOOL

The Women's Business School is a business school designed exclusively for women. Providing opportunities for innovative female founders to scale their start-up, connect with fellow founders and gain advice and guidance from successful entrepreneurs and experts. Through the award winning incubator and accelerator programs, founders receive world-class entrepreneurial education from a team of high-level experts and entrepreneurs as well as mentoring, advice and access to successful female entrepreneurs across a range of industries. If you're ready to take your business to the next level apply today!

www.thewomensbusinessschool.com

ABOUT AUSMUMPRENEUR

Australia's #1 Community for Mumpreneurs. The AusMumpreneur Awards are a national event recognising and celebrating Australia's best and brightest mums in business. Held annually these awards recognise the incredible women who are balancing business and motherhood and creating innovative, high quality and remarkable brands across a range of industries.

www.ausmumpreneur.com

ABOUT WOMEN CHANGING THE WORLD PRESS

Women Changing the World press publishes thought leaders, female founders and women who are committed to making the world a better place through their words and actions. We believe that investing in women is the most powerful way to change the world and we are passionate about amplifying women's voices, stories and ideas and providing more opportunities for women to share their message with the world. If you have a story that the world needs to hear get in touch today.

www.wcwpress.com

ABOUT WOMEN CHANGING THE WORLD INVESTMENTS

At Women Changing the World Investments our mission is to revolutionise the way women founders can access capital to grow their businesses and in turn grow their communities of influence. Investing in women, their ideas and their innovation is the way we make real change in the world.

We are committed to:
- changing the experiences and trajectory of funding for female founders and entrepreneurs
- advancing the normalisation of funding female founders
- ensuring all women have a seat at the table especially women of colour, First Nations women, women with disabilities and those who identify as women
- and changing the tone of the conversation about capital raising for female founders.

We do this through:
- Providing real, appropriate investment for female founders who share our values – when women's success is empowered and facilitated, families, communities and our society benefit.

- Providing real opportunities for investors who share our values. We also support the ambition of women to invest in viable, success-orientated businesses and be a part of growing our economy.

As part of this capital, we provide appropriate resources, connections, and skill development to ensure they are supported through their growth as a founder and the growth of their enterprise.

We are committed to creating change and incubating new opportunities for collaboration, connection, and economic growth by investing in brilliant, high-potential, women-led companies.

Our work has an immediate beneficial impact on the female founders we support, as well as creating lasting legacy work through amplifying the work of women entrepreneurs and changing the way venture capital can be accessed by women.

www.wcwinvestments.com